Advance Praise

"It's about time an informed, Bible-believing Christian explained to the growing number of skeptics and gnostics and relativists how America, the freest country in the history of the world, could only have been birthed and sustained through a Christian worldview. If you want to bring this great experiment in human liberty to a screeching halt, the fastest way is to eliminate the salt and light contributed by Divine inspiration of our heavenly Father and His Word through His children."

> —Joseph Farah
> Editor and Chief Executive Officer
> WorldNetDaily.com Inc.

"Douglas Wilson has done the near impossible. He made me glad that Sam Harris wrote his anti-God tract because it provided an occasion for Doug to write such a literate, compelling, and engaging response. I hope Bible study groups and Sunday school classes across the country set aside their normal lessons for a few weeks and gather together to study and discuss Wilson's *Letter from a Christian Citizen*."

> —Craig J. Hazen, Ph.D.
> Director, Master of Arts Program in Christian
> Apologetics, Biola University, La Mirada, California

"Douglas Wilson has written a book that can give Christians a place to stand in regard to Sam Harris' book *Letter to a Christian Nation*. The primary usefulness of Wilson's book is that it gives readers a point-by-point response to the arguments advanced by Harris in an engaging and compelling way."

> —Dr. Leland Ryken
> Professor of English at Wheaton College

"In the interaction between Doug Wilson and Sam Harris, one of them is wrong and one is right. If you can't figure it out after reading this exchange, you never will."

> —Hanna Rosin
> *Washington Post* staff writer & contributing editor,
> *The Atlantic Monthly*

Letter from a Christian Citizen

Letter from a Christian Citizen

DOUGLAS WILSON

AMERICAN VISION

POWDER SPRINGS, GEORGIA 2007

Published in the United States
and Australia by

American Vision, Inc.
3150-A Florence Rd.
Powder Springs, Georgia 30127
1-800-628-9460
www.AmericanVision.org

Library of Congress Cataloging-in-Publication Data
Wilson, Douglas
Letter from a Christian Citizen / Douglas Wilson.— 1st ed.
ISBN: 978-0-915815-75-3 (Paperback)
1. Christianity and politics—United States. 2. Church
and state—United States. 3 Fundamentalism—United
States. 4. Religious right—United States. 5. Christian
conservatism—United States. I. Title

For my wife

FOREWORD

BY GARY DEMAR

I LIKE FREE BOOKS. So I was excited when I opened a package that contained a book that I had not ordered. Apparently, I'm on someone's list of notables because Alfred A. Knopf thought I should have a copy of Sam Harris' *Letter to a Christian Nation*. And since I had received one unsolicited, surely there were others who were equally blessed with the freebie. I can't believe that anyone at Knopf thought I would be persuaded by it, so I'm assuming that an enterprising marketer saw it as a way to get some free publicity out of the gesture. It worked! And I am grateful.

There's little that's new in *Letter to a Christian Nation*. It's the old atheism wrapped in a new package. The same tired arguments that have been answered convincingly by any number of Christian writers over the centuries have been trotted out again in the vain hope that atheism will find a new audience.

Sam Harris wants to assure us that atheists aren't monsters. He's somewhat miffed that "atheists are often imagined to be intolerant, immoral, depressed, blind to the beauty of nature and dogmatically closed to evidence of the supernatural."[1] Harris is here to tell Christians, and anyone else who will listen to him, that these are mischaracterizations. This is why he feels compelled to remind his critics that "atheists are often among the most intelligent and scientifically literate people in any society."[2] Because of this, he continues, "it seems important to deflate the myths that prevent them from playing a larger role in our national discourse."

The first myth Harris wants to dispel is that "atheists believe life is meaningless." He argues that "atheists tend to be quite sure that life is precious. Life is imbued with meaning by being really and fully lived." Of course, he is arguing in a circle. How does he know when life is being really and fully lived unless he first assumes life is meaningful, the very thing he must prove as a self-avowed materialist? And how does a materialist who believes in the random origin of the universe account for meaning among the "things" that an impersonal conglomeration of atoms spontaneously brought into existence without rhyme or reason? As a letter writer to *Time* magazine put it in his response to a series of articles on the mind and body that appeared in an issue of *Time*, "I'm not sure I'll ever have the same degree of self-respect now that I know I'm just an illusion created by 100 billion jabbering neurons."[3] I suspect that any number of people—Adolf Hitler, Josef Stalin, Pol Pot, to name a few—conceptualized that they were living life to the fullest, believing that their idea of life would be more meaningful if certain people didn't share it with them.

I won't question his claim that he *believes* life is meaningful, but as an atheist Harris must account for the meaningfulness of life given the naturalistic presuppositions he shares with other prominent atheists. Consider, for example, the opening comments of John Gribbin in his book *The Scientists*. How does the atheist account for even the idea of morality when science has determined that there is no evidence "for a special 'life force' that distinguishes living matter from non-living matter"?:

> *The most important thing that science has taught us about our place in the Universe is that we are not special. . . . [B]iologists tried and failed to find any evidence for a special 'life force' that distinguishes living matter from non-living matter, concluding that life is just a rather complicated form of chemistry. . . . For human life turned out to be no different from any other kind of life on Earth. As the work of Charles Darwin and Alfred Wallace established in the nineteenth century, all you need to make human beings out of amoebas is the process of evolution by natural selection, and plenty of time.*[4]

According to Gribbin, at the biological level, science has not been able to distinguish between a human and a hammer. Both can only be studied in terms of their chemical makeup as determined by the Periodic Table. So then, the burden of proof is on Harris and all atheists to account for "meaning" given the materialistic assumptions of Gribbin and an atheist like Richard Dawkins:

> *In the universe of blind physical forces and genetic replication, some people are going to get hurt, and other people are going to get lucky; and you won't find any rhyme or reason to it, nor any justice. The universe we observe has precisely the properties we should expect if there is at the bottom, no design, no purpose, no evil and no good. Nothing but blind pitiless indifference. DNA neither knows nor cares. DNA just is, and we dance to its music.*[5]

I've brought Dawkins into the discussion because Harris puts Dawkins' *The God Delusion* on his "Ten Books I Recommend" list. Since, according to Gribbin and Dawkins, humans are composed of "a rather complicated form of chemistry" that "neither knows nor cares," logic leads to the inevitable conclusion that humans themselves should "neither know nor care." Life, therefore, given naturalistic assumptions, is by definition meaningless, or, at best, randomly confusing.

In his religious ode to evolution, *River Out of Eden*, Dawkins relates how "the British newspapers all carried a terrible story about a bus full of children from a Roman Catholic school that crashed for no obvious reason, with wholesale loss of life." He reports that a priest responded to the tragedy by stating, "But the horror of the crash, to a Christian, confirms the fact that we live in a world of real values: positive and negative. If the universe was just electrons, there would be no problem of evil or suffering."[6] Dawkins offered the following response: "On the contrary, if the universe were just electrons and selfish genes, meaningless tragedies like the crashing of this bus are exactly what we should expect, along with meaningless good fortune."[7]

How can Dawkins refer to the bus crash as "terrible" and a "tragedy"? Was he referring to the death of the children or the destruction of the bus? In Dawkins' view, there is no difference between the competing chemical entities, one consisting of electrical impulses passing through meat and bones (the children) and the other of electrical charges surging through generators and wiring (the bus).

Of course, like most of the rest of us, Dawkins does not live consistently with his own belief that Darwin's natural selection is "blind, unconscious, automatic" and with "no purpose in mind."[8] His inconsistency keeps him from being the monster he ought to be if he was a faithful practitioner of the Darwinism he promotes and defends.

We are thankful that most atheists aren't consistent with their atheistic assumptions. There have been enough who were consistent that made the twentieth century the most bloody century in history. Some saw the ramifications of a consistent atheism before it manifested itself in gulags, pogroms, and a holocaust. Southern Presbyterian theologian Robert Lewis Dabney (1820–1898) describes the atheist's dilemma by pointing out that a person's starting point leads to an inevitable conclusion:

> To borrow [Thomas] Carlyle's rough phrasing: "If mine is a pig's destiny, why may I not hold this 'pig philosophy'?"

Again, if I am but an animal refined
by evolution, I am entitled to live an
animal life. Why not? The leaders in
this and the sensualistic philosophy may
themselves be restrained by their habits
of mental culture, social discretion and
personal refinement (for which they are
indebted to reflex Christian influences);
but the herd of common mortals are not
cultured and refined, and in them the
doctrine will bear its deadly fruit.[9]

Because Christianity had so impacted nine-teenth-century society, as it still does today to the benefit of all (including atheists), the ethical and cultural effects of Darwinism were at first minimal. In time, however, as consistency began to be demanded of the new naturalistic worldview, the evolutionary dogma impacted the world in ominous ways. Today's non-monster atheists like Harris and Dawkins have been caught in the matrix of a Christian worldview that they cannot escape. If they ever do, they will join the ranks of Monsters, Inc., whose members were consis-tent with their atheistic presuppositions and unleashed untold hardship on the twentieth century.

When confronted with the charge that "atheism is responsible for the greatest crimes in human history," Mr. Harris dodges the accusation by claiming that atheist regimes like fascism and communism "are too much like religions." He's closer to the truth than he realizes. The ideological engine of atheism is evolution, and by the declaration of its own practitioners, it's a religion, as evolutionary apologist Michael Ruse makes very clear: "Evolution is a religion. This was true of evolution in the beginning, and it is true of evolution still today."[10]

Ruse is not alone in his admission that evolution is a materialistic religion founded on, as far as I've been able to determine, unaccounted for metaphysical assumptions. "The distinguished biologist Lynn Margulis has rather scathingly referred to new-Darwinism as 'a minor twentieth century religious sect within the sprawling religious persuasion of Anglo-Saxon biology.' Stuart Kauffman observes that 'natural selection' has become so central an explanatory force in neo-Darwinism

LETTER FROM A CHRISTIAN CITIZEN

that 'we might as well capitalise [it] as though it were the new deity.'"[11]

When Dawkins was asked, "What do you believe that you cannot prove?," he admitted the following: "I believe, but I cannot prove, that all life, all intelligence, all creativity and all 'design' anywhere in the universe, is the direct or indirect product of Darwinian natural selection."[12] Dawkins, and those who follow his naturalistic creed, have faith in an impersonal cosmos that is the product of a faith-committed impersonal concept that has no inherent moral brake.

The atrocities of Josef Stalin and Adolf Hitler reveal in stark detail how despotic and cruel the impersonal worldview of naturalism can be if followed consistently. It is no accident that Communism and Nazism claimed Darwin as their patron saint. Darwin's approach to origins found an enthusiastic adherent in Karl Marx and his communist successors. Marx wrote to Friedrich Engels in 1866 that Darwin's *Origin of Species* "is the book which contains the basis in natural history for our view."[13] There are no absolutes, man is nothing, and the State is everything. For Communism, the advancement of the State is the march of god on earth. Communism ensures this through raw power, the Gulag, and the "necessary" extinction of millions to bring the "ideals" of Communism to the masses.[14]

> *The scientific racism of Nazi Germany killed forty million and attempted genocide against Europe's Jews. The scientific socialism of the Communist countries killed a hundred million (and still counting) people around the globe. As the Soviet dissident Vladimir Bukovsky has noted, people in the West routinely invoke the Spanish Inquisition as an example of religious horror. And they are right to do so. But the Inquisition, in the course of three centuries, and after legal procedures of a sort, killed fewer people—probably around three thousand—than the Soviet Union killed on an average day.*[15]

Douglas Wilson has taken the operating assumptions of Sam Harris seriously and has shown what life would be like if the world were consistent with atheistic assumptions. He deals a final blow to Harris by pointing out that the morality he values is borrowed moral capital. What he knows of right and wrong does not flower from atheistic roots.

Letter From a Christian Citizen will prove to be a painful exercise for any atheist since it exposes the raw nerve of materialism—the desire for a moral worldview that cannot be accounted for given naturalistic assumptions. "We make men without chests and we expect of them virtue and enterprise," C.S. Lewis writes. "We laugh at honor and we are shocked to find traitors in our midst. We castrate and bid the geldings be fruitful."[16] We strip men and women of the certainty that they are created in the image of God, and we are surprised when they act like the beasts of the field.

NOTES

[1]Sam Harris, "Atheists surely aren't monsters," *The Atlanta Journal-Constitution* (December 28, 2006), A21. All the quotations from Harris in the Foreword are from this article.

[2]I'm not sure if Harris means by this comment that theists are neither intelligent nor scientifically minded. If this is his intent, then he needs a short course in the history of science. Science developed within the context of a Christian worldview. See Nancy R. Pearcey and Charles B. Thaxton, *The Soul of Science: Christian Faith and Natural Philosophy* (Wheaton, IL: Crossway Books, 1994); R. Hooykaas, *Religion and the Rise of Modern Science* (Grand Rapids, MI: Eerdmans, 1972); Eugene M. Klaaren, *Religious Origins of Modern Science* (Grand Rapids, MI: Eerdmans, 1977); Stanley L. Jaki, *The Origin of Science and the Science of Its Origin* (South Bend, IN: Regnery/Gateway, Inc., 1978); Stanley L. Jaki, *The Savior of Science* (Washington, DC: Regnery, 1988); Gary DeMar, *Whoever Controls the Schools Rules the World* (Powder Springs, GA: American Vision, 2007).

[3]Gregory Dobbins, "Letters," *Time* (February 12, 2007), 18. The letter was a response to "Mind and Body Special Issue," *Time* (January 29, 2007).

[4]John Gribbin, *The Scientists: A History of Science Told through the Lives of its Greatest Inventors* (New York: Random House, [2002] 2006), xvii, ix.

[5]Richard Dawkins, *River Out of Eden: A Darwinian View of Life* (New York: HarperCollins/BasicBooks, 1995), 133.

[6]Dawkins, *River Out of Eden*, 132.

[7]Dawkins, *River Out of Eden*, 132.

[8]Richard Dawkins, *The Blind Watchmaker: Why the Evidence of Evolution Reveals a Universe without Design* (New York: Norton, 1986), 5. For a refutation of T*he Blind Watchmaker,* see Neil Broom, *How Blind is the Watchmaker? Nature's Design and the Limits of Naturalistic Science* (Downers Grove, IL: InterVarsity Press, 1998.

[9]Robert L. Dabney, "The Influences of False Philosophies upon Character and Conduct," in *Discourses* (Harrisonburg, VA: Sprinkle Pub., 1979), 4:574.

[10]Michael Ruse, "Saving Darwinism from the Darwinians," *National Post* (May 13, 2000), B3.

[11] Philip J. Sampson, *6 Modern Myths About Christianity and Western Civilization* (Downers Grove, IL: InterVarsity Press, 2001), 62.

[12] "God (or Not), Physics and, of Course, Love: Scientists Take a Leap," *The New York Times* (January 4, 2005). Quoted in Robert Royal, *The God that Did Not Fail: How Religion Built and Sustains the West* (New York: Encounter Books, 2006), xii.

[13] R. L. Meek, ed., *Marx and Engels on Malthus* (New York: International Publishers, 1954), 171. Quoted in Michael Pitman, *Adam and Evolution* (London, England: Rider & Company, 1984), 24.

[14] Mark Kramer, ed., *The Black Book of Communism: Crimes, Terror, Repression,* trans. Jonathan Murphy and Mark Kramer (Cambridge, MA: Harvard University Press, 1999); *Robert Conquest, The Great Terror: A Reassessment* (New York: Oxford University Press, 1990); and Lloyd Billingsly, *The Generation that Knew Not Josef: A Critique of Marxism and the Religious Left* (Portland, OR: Multnomah Press, 1985).

[15] Royal, *The God that Did Not Fail*, xvii.

[16] C. S. Lewis, *The Abolition of Man* (New York: Macmillan, [1947] 1972), 35.

Letter From a Christian Citizen:

A REPLY TO SAM HARRIS

Dear Mr. Harris

I WOULD LOVE TO begin by saying something like "Greetings in the Lord," but I have no idea what your background is or whether you have ever been baptized. And so, not to presume, let me begin simply by greeting you warmly in a general fashion and thanking you for setting your thoughts down so plainly. I would also hope that I might raise some equally clear questions about what you have written.

On the first page of your small book, you begin by discussing some of the reaction you got to your first book, *The End of Faith*. You say that the "most hostile" responses came to you from Christians. "The truth is that many who claim to be transformed by Christ's love are deeply, even murderously, intolerant of criticism" (vii). You suggest the possibility that this might just be attributable to human nature, but you don't think so. You go on to suggest that "such hatred" draws "considerable support from the Bible." You say your reason for saying this is that the "most disturbed of my correspondents always cite chapter and verse" (vii).

I think I know why you began your book this way. I have been in evangelical Christian circles my entire life, and one of the *standard* concerns that many Christians have is presenting "a bad testimony" to nonbelievers. Of course this doesn't prevent some Christians from presenting that bad testimony anyway, oblivious to all surrounding concerns. But your opening is guaranteed to cause many Christian readers to lament the fact that a number of professing Christians have sought to clobber you for Christ through their hostility. And then when you didn't respond favorably to "the treatment," these sorts of people have another chapter and verse handy that can explain *that*.

You opened your book this way because you knew (quite accurately) that Christians generally would be upset by it, would be put on the defensive, would be sorrowful over what some have done to you in the name of Christ,

4

and so on. I know, and you clearly know, that Christians can behave badly in this way, and you also knew that a lot of other Christians would be ashamed of this undeniable fact. And you are right: We are ashamed of this kind of thing. Like you, I've had first-hand experience. When my son (a Christian) published an article showing how the Shroud of Turin could easily have been produced with medieval "off-the-shelf" technology,[1] he got lots of mail—from professing Christians—with all sorts of variants of "go to hell" or "I hope you rot in hell."

The Christian Church has a problem with this kind of person in our midst. We are embarrassed by it, believing it to be inconsistent with what Christ taught and what we profess to believe. Attributing it to human nature doesn't cut it with us because we believe that Christ came to transform human nature. You knew this about us and started out very shrewdly. You knew that we would disapprove of this kind of thing, just as you do.

But *that*, actually, was the surprising thing: you disapproved of that kind of hateful behavior too. You used a number of words that clearly portrayed that disapproval: *hostile, murderously, disturbed, hatred.* I could not get to your second page without encountering a cluster of indignant moral judgments, and I am genuinely curious as to what you could possibly offer as the basis for these judgments. Pick the nastiest letter you got from the nastiest Christian out there. As a pastor, I know what *I* would say to him about it because I can appeal to the Bible. But what could *you* say to him? He is just doing his thing. Two hundred years from now, when both you and he have returned to the soil, what difference will it make? There is no judgment, no standard, no law that overarches the two of you. When this nasty Christian dies, you don't even have the satisfaction of knowing that he will finally discover the error of his ways. He will discover nothing of the kind. You believe his eyes will close and that will be that. The material universe will not give everyone thirty minutes after death to readjust their thoughts on the subject before they pass into final oblivion. So why, on your terms, should he have written you a nice letter? *I* think he should have, but then again, I'm the pastor guy.

In different ways this same issue is going to come up again and again as I respond to different portions of your book. You want Christians to quit behaving in certain ways. But why? You want them to write nice letters to atheist authors, and you want them to stop turning America into a big, dumb theocracy. But *why*? If there is no God, what could *possibly* be wrong with theocracies? They provide high entertainment value, and they give everybody involved in them a sense of dignity and high moral purpose. They get to wear ecclesiastical robes, march in impressive processions to burn intransigent people at the stake, believing they are better than everybody else and that God likes them. Further, the material universe doesn't care about any of this foolishness, not even a little bit. So what's wrong with having a little bit of fun at the expense of other bits of protoplasm? Hitler, Ronald Reagan, Pol Pot, Mother Teresa, Mao, Nancy Pelosi, Stalin, Ted Haggard, and the Grand Inquisitor are all just part of a gaudy and very temporary show. Sometimes the Northern lights put on a show in the sky. Sometimes people put on a show on the ground. Then the sun goes out and it turns out nobody cares. Given your premises, this is the way it has to be.

But I find it really curious that you clearly do care what happens to our nation. "The primary purpose of the book is to arm secularists in our society, who believe that religion should be kept out of public policy, against their opponents on the Christian Right" (viii). Again, you are using words like *should be*. Not only do you have an *ought* going here, you have one that you are clearly willing to impose on others who differ with you (which can be seen in your goal of "arming" secularists). But what is the difference between an imposed morality, an imposed religion, or an imposed secular *ought*? Why is your imposition to be preferred to any other?

Although your book is small, the goal is certainly ambitious. "In *Letter to a Christian Nation*, I have set out to demolish the intellectual and moral pretensions of Christianity in its most committed forms" (ix). In order to demolish something intellectually, you have to have a standard for thought and reason and I presume you will reveal this standard later in your book so we will be able to discuss it. But you also want to demolish the moral pretensions of the Christian faith. This could have two meanings. You might mean to show that Christianity does not live up to its own professed standard, in which case you are simply joining a long covenant tradition which includes the prophet Amos and John the Baptist. I could not really object to this because it is what I try to do every Sunday in the pulpit. But you appear to mean something else. You seem to be saying that there is a standard which Christianity does not acknowledge even though it is authoritative over Christians anyway, and that Christianity is in rebellion against this standard. I want to continue to ask you for the source of this standard. Who has defined this standard? You? Your friends? Is it published somewhere so I can read it? You write as though it exists. Where is it?

You say, "In *Letter to a Christian Nation*, however, I engage Christianity at its most divisive, injurious, and retrograde" (ix). So Christianity is divisive, compared to what standard for unity? Who promulgated this standard? Why do we have to submit to it?

Christianity is injurious, you say, but I would want to inquire why it is bad to be injurious. What standard do you appeal to here? And *retrograde* means that we are sliding backwards in some sense. What slope are we sliding down? Why are we not allowed to slide down it? I am not trying to be cute here. I think these are the central questions in this discussion. Okay, so I am part of a *divisive*, *injurious* and *retrograde* movement. Is that bad?

At the conclusion of your "Note to the Reader," you make an opening move in what I suppose is part of your larger strategy of demolishing the "intellectual pretensions of Christianity." You begin by noting that the intellectual pretensions of the Christian faith are certainly widespread. "If our worldview were put to a vote, notions of 'intelligent design' would defeat the science of biology by nearly three to one" (x). I do not share the same faith you apparently do in the abilities of pollsters to measure this sort of thing, but let us grant this as at least a distinct possibility. You believe that the pervasiveness of certain Christian doctrines constitutes "a moral and intellectual emergency" (xii). You speak in terms of "us and them," so allow me to do the same thing for a moment. You all have had nearly complete control of the education establishment for over a century and a half. You have the accrediting agencies, you have the government schools, and you have the vast majority of colleges and universities. You *are* the educational establishment. And yet your complaint here reminds me of the indignant father who said, "I taught him everything I know and he's *still* stupid!" At what point should a committed secularist take responsibility for the state of education in America? Perhaps the problem is not in the students?

But there is more to this argument. It is quite true that I do not regard the widespread acceptance of intelligent design as indicating stupidity, apathy, or worse. I believe God created the world, and His intelligence is on display in riotous ways in everything I look at every day. But given the current climate, this conviction is certainly easy to *mock*— "This means that despite a full century of scientific insights attesting to the antiquity of the earth, more than half of our neighbors believe that the entire cosmos was created six thousand years ago. This is, incidentally, about a thousand years after the Sumerians invented glue" (x–xi). But notice what you are doing here: the Sumerians *invented* glue? Glue didn't just happen? Why couldn't it just appear the same way the sexuality of moss did and the eyeballs that see in color and the superbly engineered ankle and the majesty of the great white sharks all did? *Glue* is so complicated that it needed to be invented?

You say that our nation is a "dim-witted giant" (xi). You say that we combine "great power and great stupidity" (xi). To bring this installment to a close, let me just give you a friendly caution. This sort of thing is probably red meat to many of the folks buying your books. But if you are really concerned about delivering the nation from the "clutches" of Christians, I am afraid that underestimating the intelligence and education of your foes will probably not help you at all in the long run.

A Trout in the Punchbowl

In your first argument (3–7), you begin the discussion with agreement. That agreement may seem minimal to some, but I actually believe that a great deal rides on it. The agreement is that one of us must be right and the other wrong. There is either a God or there is not. As you put it, "We agree, for instance, that if one of us is right, the other is wrong. The Bible is either the word of God or it isn't. Either Jesus offers humanity the one, true path to salvation (John 14:6), or he does not" (3). This is an appropriate way to state it and a good place to begin. Some might claim this is a false dichotomy, but it really is a fair statement. If I say the car must either be red or green, I am leaving a lot of other possibilities out. But if I say the car must either be red or not red, I have pretty much covered the waterfront.

And so we agree. Jesus is either the divine Son of God or He is not. Jesus either died on the cross as a sacrifice for the sins of humanity or He did not. I will return to the implications of this in a future section.

But not surprisingly we then part company. You say, "Consider: every devout Muslim has *the same reasons* for being a Muslim that you have for being a Christian" (6, emphasis mine). You advance an argument that might be called an argument for partial atheism:

"The truth is, you know exactly what it is like to be an atheist with respect to the beliefs of Muslims" (7). But I am afraid that this is a false analogy entirely. You say, "Understand that the way you view Islam is precisely the way devout Muslims view Christianity. And it is the way I view all religions" (7). Well, no, not exactly. And well, actually, no, not at all.

Suppose we are considering a phenomenon that is, by *most* accounts, inexplicable as an unsupervised occurrence—three of us attend a sophisticated party uptown, and half way through the evening at the party we find a trout in the punch bowl. At this point, the three of us divide into three schools of thought. I think that Smith, a practical joker, put it there; our friend Murphy thinks that Jones, the *avant-garde* performance artist, put it there; and you think that it has simply shown up as the result of natural forces. My central point is not to interact with the truth or falsity of your naturalistic position—except perhaps through the use of this absurd example of the punchbowl—but rather to show that you are arguing for something *completely different* from what Murphy and I are arguing. We all have an explanation but your explanation is of a different kind altogether.

The differences between two of us (between Murphy and me) concern *who* put the trout in the punchbowl. The difference between the both of us together and you is over *whether* someone put a trout in the punchbowl. And *who* and *whether* represent different questions entirely. Quite apart from who is right and who is wrong about this, it is important to note that we are not disagreeing in the same way or over the same kind of issue at all. Murphy and I are disagreeing about the relative behaviors of Smith and Jones, but not over whether the trout calls for an explanation. Maybe I am more hostile to Smith than I ought to be, and maybe Murphy is deeply prejudiced against Jones. Maybe we are both wrong about who put it there. But thinking that someone's explanation is inadequate (when we agree the phenomenon *must* be explained) is quite different from arguing with someone who says that it calls for no outside explanation whatever.

When a general wants to fight a battle, he also wants to pick the terrain. Being able to choose the location is always a significant advantage. Likewise, the way a debate is structured will often affect the outcome of that debate. And so we need to begin our discussion by noting that your structure for this debate needs to be completely revised. Rejecting a proffered explanation is totally different from saying there is no need for an explanation. In short, your unbelief in the Christian faith is *not* the same kind of thing at all as my unbelief in Islam. And I am not a "partial atheist" because I am not a Muslim. You say, "No one needed to put the world here." The Muslim says that Allah created it. I say that the triune God did. These statements contradict one another *in different ways*—not in the same way, as you argued.

I admitted above that the trout in the punchbowl was an absurd example, but before wrapping this up, I want to make sure my admission is not taken the wrong way. I was not confessing that I was attempting a straw man argument. By such examples I am not trying to make your position *look* absurd; rather, I am trying to communicate something of the wonder Christians feel when we look at virtually anything in the real world. A trout in the punchbowl would certainly surprise me, but really no more than do hummingbird wings, the conveyor belt in our ears that slowly carries the wax out, pine cones that don't do any reproductive good until a forest fire pops them open, the carefully perforated edge around a housefly pupa that doesn't come open until a blood bag comes out of the fly's head to push it open, or an acorn that has the ability to make a huge oak tree out of what it finds in the air. The trout in the punch actually requires far less explaining than any of these things. So the absurdity of my example is actually that it falls so far short.

You might respond by saying that since the punchbowl was filled at 6:30 and we arrived at the party around 7:15, this did not give the laws of nature any *time* to do their usual magic. The evolution of life on our planet, you might say, required many millions of years to accomplish what it has. But if we are talking about matter organizing itself up a cliff face with no pitons or boots at a strenuous climb, additional time only makes the problems worse. Miracles don't go any better if you roll the tape in slow motion. Ice cubes bumping together won't make a trout, and I can't evade the difficulties inherent in the theory by postulating an additional one hundred years for the ice cubes to bump in. If I wanted to walk across the swimming pool, I do not increase my chances by inching out onto the water *slowly*. This means that your account of the trout in the punchbowl is tenuous whether you have a lot of time or not very much time.

But in *either* case, whether we are dealing with eons or minutes, your naturalistic explanation of how a trout might have gotten there remains a very different kind of explanation than those given by people who believe *someone* had to put it there.

Playing to the Cheap Seats

Your next argument does not appear to be a proper argument at all, but rather a marshalling of "scary quotes" from the Old Testament. These are set against certain contemporary assumptions about law and justice, and you do this on the safe bet that most of your readers will not go back and question any of those assumptions. But I think it would be really helpful if someone were actually to do that.

Some of your assumptions do not appear to have been asked a question in years.

You cite various biblical laws that have offended your sensibilities (Prov. 13:24; 20:30; 23:13–14; Ex. 21:15; Lev. 20:9; Deut. 21:18–21; Mark 7:9–13; Matt. 15:4–7; Deut. 13:6, 8–15). You point out (quite *correctly*, I might add) that Jesus was not in the least bit embarrassed by any of this. You cite Matthew 5:18–19 to establish this point, but it would have strengthened your argument significantly to use Mark 7:10 where Jesus expressly refers to one of the "scary parts" of the Old Testament (the penalty for cursing parents), and He does so with an unapologetic affirmation.[2]

You cite 2 Thessalonians 1:6–9 and John 15:6 to show (again rightly) that the New Testament does not represent what could be called a softening of the ethics of the Old Testament. Grace and love and supreme kindness characterize the New Testament, that is true, but these are also found in the Old Testament. Law and judgment are indeed found in the Old Testament, but these are found in *heightened* form in the New Testament. So you are correct. It is false to say that the Old Testament represents "severity" and the New Testament represents "kindness." Both are found in the Old Testament, and both are found in accentuated form in the New Testament. The judgments that fall in the Old Testament are largely temporal judgments. The judgments that Jesus speaks of are eternal. Out of all the teachers and prophets in the Bible, the preeminent hellfire and damnation preacher is the Lord Jesus Himself. You rightly see that the Old and New Testaments stand or fall together.

But then, instead of demonstrating why they must *fall* together, you simply make an appeal to the nickel seats. You bring up laws and customs involving cultures thousands of years away from us, and you use the "outlandish" aspects of these customs to frighten modernists who don't get out much. For example, without providing any context you cite a passage that you say allows a father to sell his daughter "into sexual slavery" (Ex. 21:7–11). But what this law actually represents is an amelioration of an existing custom, and the law placed bounds and restrictions on that custom to keep abuses from becoming outrages. The same kind of thing happened with polygamy—not approved as such, but restricted and bounded.

But while we are on the subject of sexual slavery, let me raise the question whether anything like that is occurring now. Are there fathers who pimp their daughters today? Well, yes, but when it happens, we are probably talking about an MTV reality show and the general approval from the fans of cultural degradation. But if that is not explicit enough, then let's talk about sexual slavery of *children* in places like Thailand. And let's ask who would be most likely to approve of sexual jaunts to visit the slaves there—your average believer in the Old Testament laws you dismissively cite or people who share your opinions about the reject status of Old Testament law? Are there special airfare rates from San Francisco do you think?

You didn't limit your discussion to sexual slavery though. You gave us several passages where the apostle Paul "admonishes slaves to serve their masters well—and to serve their Christian masters especially well" (16). You cite Ephesians 6:5 and 1 Timothy 6:1–4 which make your point plainly enough. Unlike some of the Old Testament passages you cited, your representation of these passages was fairly accurate. St. Paul *did* teach Christian slaves to work hard. He taught Christian masters to remember that they had a master in heaven, and this presupposes that there were Christian masters who were members of his churches. He did teach Christian slaves to make a special point of working diligently for believing masters. Now here is my question. Given your worldview, what is wrong with this? There is nothing wrong with it on your principles, where the universe is just time and chance acting on matter. Why does it matter if the master matter acts on the slave matter? Who cares?

From our Christian perspective, the apostle was subverting the *entire* pagan system—and taking it down with the pagan system of slavery included in the demolition job. He did not do this by revolutionary means, but rather by means of the Christian gospel. Biblical subversion of pagan slavery was not violent, but rather worked the same way that yeast works through a loaf of bread. Promoting the ethic of a new world, a new heaven and a new earth, was what the apostle Paul was after, and slavery was radically inconsistent with this vision. A very good description of the Pauline strategy in this can be found in N.T. Wright's commentary on Philemon, the letter in which Paul is returning a runaway slave.[3]

But from an atheistic perspective, how can slavery be consistently condemned? You don't really address this question at all, but rather engage in some ethical hand waving. "Nothing in Christian theology remedies the appalling deficiencies of the Bible on what is perhaps the greatest—and the *easiest*—moral question our society has ever had to face" (18). All right. You say this is the easiest moral question that our society has ever faced. Okay then, that sounded confident. This must be a *really* easy question for you to answer. You asserted this, but then you did not answer it. Given your principles, why is slavery wrong? The Christian view is that all mankind is created in the image of God, and that Christ came to liberate us from our slavery to sin and restore that image. It is easy to see on these principles how slavery is not what God intends for us. Christ came to proclaim liberty for the captives

(Luke 4:18). The Bible prohibits the man-stealing that was the foundation of the slave trade (1 Tim. 1:10). In Christ there is neither Jew nor Greek, male or female, slave or free (Gal. 3:28). The logic of the new creation in Christ provides liberation from the slavery of sin which is the foundation of all other forms of slavery (Gal. 5:1). But how could *atheism* lead to a condemnation of slavery?

You make a superficial attempt to answer the question, but it really answers nothing, and addresses nothing. "The moment a person recognizes that slaves are human beings like himself, enjoying the same capacity for suffering and happiness, he will understand that it is patently evil to own them and treat them like farm equipment" (18–19). This appears to be an argument that nerve endings disqualify one from being a slave or being treated like farm equipment. But what about farm *animals*? They have nerve endings, and they certainly have a capacity for suffering. This anticipates the problem you have with your approval of Jain ethics, but I will address this shortly.

Secondly, you simply throw random texts at your readers and expect them to react with indignation. This is easy to do because in Old Testament societies, when criminal or financial offenses were committed, the options that they had were execution, exile, fines, flogging, and slavery. These options are there, right in the text. But out of this list of five, we still practice three of them in our nation today—execution, fines, and slavery. If a non-citizen is involved, we still practice a fourth—exile (calling it deportation). The only sentence that is not used in our nation today is flogging.

You might object to my assertion that we still have slavery. But notice what our Constitution says about it. "Neither slavery nor involuntary servitude, *except as a punishment* for crime whereof the party shall have been duly convicted, shall exist within the United States, or any place subject to their jurisdiction" (Art. XIII, sec. 1, emphasis mine). And this is not a punishment that we resort to on rare occasions either. There are over two *million* people currently incarcerated in the United States. You think that slavery is gone because on your way to work you don't drive by anybody working in the cotton fields. That is because *our* system of slavery has built a massive network of kennels to store people out of sight in six-foot by eight-foot cells. You might say that these people are restricted in their liberty because they were convicted of crimes. Many of them were, and every society has a right to protect itself—ours included— and so perhaps you ought not to ride a high horse when it comes to ancient societies protecting themselves as well.

But even with allowances made in this way, I want to press the point—we are not dealing with two million murderers, rapists, or violent offenders. Quite a few of the inhabitants of these secularist kennels of yours were idiot teenagers with a bag of pot. Many others have been incarcerated for property crimes. While the Bible mandates that they pay restitution to the victims, our "modern-day" criminal justice system sends them to graduate schools of crime and vice from courtrooms that are as secular as anything someone like you could desire. In these courtrooms, if an attorney were to quote the Ten Commandments or the Golden Rule with any kind of approval, the judge would voice strong and immediate disapproval. You told us that this was an easy moral question. Why haven't we solved it yet? Why does the United States house two million slaves? That is *twice* the entire population of the state I live in. Given this, your easy dismissal of biblical ethics is just that—far too easy. "Anyone who believes the Bible offers the best guidance we have on questions of morality has some very strange ideas about either guidance or morality" (14).

This brings us back to your basis for morality, which was basically pleasure and pain. "Questions of morality are questions about happiness and suffering. This is why you and I do not have moral obligations toward rocks" (8). Okay. *Whose* happiness and suffering? Why ought one individual, with one set of nerve endings, be concerned about another set of nerve endings entirely? They are not connected, except through cultural teaching. That teaching, in our case, is grounded in the will of God. In your case, it is grounded in bare assertion. What you need to do here is sketch for us the bridge between one set of nerve endings and another, and show us why that bridge of yours creates an obligation those two sets of nerve endings must share. You say this is obvious, so it should not take that long to explain. "There are obvious biological reasons why people tend to treat their parents well, and to think badly of murderers, adulterers, thieves, and liars" (21). Obvious biological reasons? A mother's day card proceeds from the same kind of impulse that causes me to scratch an itch or go to the bathroom? *Biological* reasons? There are also obvious biological reasons that might run the other way, that go into adultery, for example. You really need to explain this further.

One last thing. You refer to the "obscene celebrations of violence that we find throughout the Old and New Testaments" (11). You set this over against the "utter non-violence" of Jainism, a religion originating in ancient India which you praise highly. This is frankly mystifying. You say the morality of the Jains surpasses the morality of the Christians, and you cite a Jain tenet. "Do not injure, abuse, oppress, enslave, insult, torment, torture, or kill any creature or living being" (23). I really cannot figure this out. You are an atheist, an *evolutionist*. And yet you praise the morality of utter non-violence, which would have gotten the evolutionary struggle absolutely nowhere. Devout Jains will go barefoot all the time to avoid stepping on bugs, and will carry a broom to sweep the path in front of them all the time, for the same reason. Devout Jains will wear a mask to avoid breathing in and thereby killing any insect. You say this represents a superior morality to that of the Christians who believe in the Bible. So you are saying— as an atheist—that if America's evangelical Christians all forsook the use of antibiotics because of the genocidal devastation it was causing to the microbes within, you would *commend* us for the moral advance? Do you promise? Because it seems to me that it would be a golden opportunity for you to dismiss us all as uneducated nutjobs.

This is a response to just a few pages from your book, and it represents one of the central problems that I see in how you are arguing your case. You are raising far more questions than you are answering, and yet you are raising them as though they were already answered.

And I think this, again, is just playing to the cheap seats.

So What's Wrong With Tin Foil Ice Cream?

I was very interested in your section called "Real Morality" (23–32) because I believe that atheism is at its weakest when it comes to finding a decent foundation for *oughts* and *shoulds*. In this section you sought to establish an objective basis for morality apart from the authority of a divine being. In addition to this, you sought to critique various aspects of Christian morality. Not surprisingly, I believe your argument failed on both counts.

Your critique of Christian morality is what I would like to deal with first, because your critique involved some astounding internal contradictions. For example, you attack the evangelical opposition to embryonic stem cell research. "A three-day-old human embryo is a collection of 150 cells called a blastocyst" (29). You compared this to the number of cells in a common household fly and ridiculed evangelical deficiencies when it came to moral proportionality. Now I differ with this criticism but it is at least a cogent argument. But what I could not reconcile was this critique with your earlier praise of the Jains in the previous section. You commended them for their commitment to *absolute* non-violence. As I mentioned, devout Jains will sweep the walk in front of them to keep from killing the bugs. Their commitment to non-violence includes a commitment to non-violence against, say, malarial mosquitoes. You imply that if evangelicals would get behind the medical use of embryonic stem cells, then much greater good would come of it. (By the way, I am here concerned simply with the *structure* of your argument. Whether the "promise" of embryonic stem cell research can live up to the current whooping for funding is a question for another time.) But why are the Jains not condemned for this same reason? Why is their unwillingness to take out mosquitoes on a par with the evangelical respect for the life of the blastocyst? Why do you not praise the evangelicals for taking a small step, however small, toward a universal respect for all life? Just like the Jains?

Your inconsistency here is why you could say something like this: "This explains why Christians like yourself expend more 'moral' energy opposing abortion than fighting genocide" (25). Please know that to Christian ears a statement like this sounds like: "When are you Christians going to stop defending Jews and join us in opposing the *real* holocausts around the globe?" Such a statement would reveal perhaps more than the speaker intended, implying that killing Jews does not qualify as a real holocaust. On Christian terms opposing abortion *is* fighting genocide. When you chide us for fighting abortion instead of genocide you reveal your assumption that unborn children are not human beings—for if they were, killing them by the millions would be genocide, would it not?

But even on Jain terms, praised highly by you just a few pages earlier, abortion can certainly be opposed because our respect should extend to "any creature or living being." Your moral calculus has been cast thus far in terms of advancing happiness and avoiding pain and suffering. You praised, in glowing terms, the length to which Jains would go to avoid doing injury to *any* living creature. We saw that this includes wearing face masks to avoid breathing in a bug. Now would you care to compare the suffering of a breathed-in bug to the suffering of a late term fetus, the victim of a partial birth abortion? And would you care to explain why you call Christians fanatics for opposing such slaughter of unborn children, but point to Jains as moral exemplars for protecting bugs?

You mock Christian concerns over the human soul, reducing it to a question of *size*. "The naive idea of souls in a Petri dish is intellectually indefensible . . . Your beliefs about the human soul are, at this very moment, prolonging the scarcely endurable misery of tens of millions of human beings" (31). There are two problems here. First, in blunt terms, you are prepared to sacrifice the small for the sake of the large, not having learned the important lessons taught by *Horton Hears a Who*, which is, that a "person's a person, no matter how small." But at the same time this oversight is not consistent at all. You are prepared to praise those who defend the small, provided that defender is not a Christian. This betrays your prejudice against Christians, regardless of what they do. It appears that your interest is to throw something at the Christians, and you don't really seem to mind what it is so long as it's hard.

The second problem is that you engaged in a little sleight of hand here. You don't believe in the human soul in the Petri dish, that's true enough. But you also don't believe in the human soul when it is encased in one J.S. Bach and is busy composing *The Brandenburg Concertos*. You make as though it is incredible to believe that a small cluster of cells can be ensouled, but your real issue is that you believe that no one has a soul. Right? We are all bags of complex chemical reactions—whether 150 cells or 10 trillion of them is just a matter of how big the sack is. But then you demand to know why we won't sacrifice the blastocysts for the sake "tens of millions of human beings." Human beings? What are those?

Your book so far has been filled with many moral judgments and assessments, and given your denial of God's existence, how you justify this is a matter of some interest. Your basis for objective morality (without God) basically amounts to an appeal to the capacity for happiness and pain respectively. "For there to be objective moral truths worth knowing, there need only be better and worse ways to seek happiness in this world" (23). But in order for this moral calculus to work, it has to be aligned with what it is based on. If it is based on the nervous system and the capacity for pain and pleasure, then it extends just as far as that nervous system does and no further. A moral standard contrary to what brings one nervous system pleasure is a standard that can be rejected by *that* nervous system out of hand. You try to say that love is better than hate, all things considered. But this is like saying that since most people like vanilla ice cream, manufacturers make far more vanilla than the kind that has chunks of tin foil in it. Okay. But making "the ice cream less eaten" would not be a *moral* issue. It is just a question of what most people like. Not only is this so, but we could also point out that in certain portions of the world, the tin foil ice cream appears to be enjoying robust sales.

This is how you describe it. "Everything about human experience suggests that love is more conducive to happiness than hate is. This is an objective claim about the human mind, about the dynamics of social relations, and about the moral order of our world" (24).

But three questions come to mind. First, why is this not a question of preferences, instead of morality? What's the difference between individual preferences and moral choices? Second, if "everything about human experience" shows that love is better than hate, why is there so much hate? Why are people buying the tin foil ice cream? And third, why do you appeal to the broad range of human experience when it comes to love and hate, and feel free to reject the broad range of human experience in its denial of atheism?

I am genuinely interested to hear your explanation of your double standard when it comes to Christians and Jains. And I would really like to hear how you bridge the gap between nervous systems (where *all* pain and pleasure is experienced) without resorting to the market of collective choices (which has no pain or pleasure). And even if you get to the market, this reduces all questions of morality to a matter of consumer choice. And how is that morality?

Douglas Wilson

The Great Jacuzzi of Consumerism

Your next section is comparatively short, and I believe this response will also be. In "Doing Good for God," you grant that Christians have often done good in the world, but that they have been restricted by their dogmas, which have greatly hampered them. In contrast to this, you hold forth the far better example of secular philanthropists, who are untrammeled by any restrictive doctrines. For an example of the former, you admire Mother Teresa (*kind* of), but then say that she was encumbered by the heavy weight of her dogmatic religious convictions.

Here we Christians are distracted by issues like abortion when there are all these other situations we could be doing something about. "At this very moment, millions of sentient people are suffering unimaginable physical and mental afflictions, in circumstances where the compassion of God is nowhere to be seen, and the compassion of human beings is often hobbled by preposterous ideas about sin and salvation" (37). Every time you speak this way, I want to bring you back to the fundamental question about suffering. Given your principles, what is wrong with it? If I am living here in North America and my nervous system is not wired up to those who are suffering in Africa, given your principles, why should I care? If ten people die in agony on the other side of the world, or if ten million do, if the word never gets to me, and the pain never registers in me, then why should I care?

Don't get me wrong. I believe we *must* care . . . because we are all created in the image of God, and Christ died for all the nations of men. But you would call this just one of my silly superstitions. Christ told us that we were to take the gospel to every creature, and this includes those cultural blessings that the gospel brings with it. But that's what I think. I am asking *you* why pain that never registers as pain *in me* brings any moral obligation to me. In addition, if I am living here in North America, that great Jacuzzi of consumerism, and enjoying the heck out of it, then why should I surrender all that in order to go suffer through what it takes to bring some relief to others? Who cares? Before I cared, no pain in me. After I cared, lots of pain in me. Please explain to me why I should exchange pleasure for pain in the only place where pleasure and pain register. Why are pleasure and absence of suffering the highest good? And if they *are* the highest good, then how can we possibly get to a collective morality when human societies don't have nerve endings?

You are assuming a great solidarity of nervous systems, and I do not see how collective moral obligation can arise out of this—particularly since the pain and pleasure calculus you use does not jump from one nervous system to another. On top of that, what gives pleasure to certain sub-groups of human nervous systems gives pain to other sub-groups. How are we to sort this out? If pain and pleasure are the real things that count, it would seem that we have to side with the bigger tribe because they are carrying around more nerve endings. They would experience more pleasure and the defeated tribe would experience less pain. And after the genocide the defeated tribe would experience *no* pain. So as far as the atheist is concerned, that problem is permanently solved and we have ourselves a final solution. I know that you are appalled by this kind of reasoning and say that it does not represent your thinking, which I grant. But I want to know *why* it does not represent your thinking. Why do you assume a solidarity of all humankind as opposed to a tribal or racial solidarity? To what objective standard do you appeal for your code of conduct?

One other brief comment. You point out that many abortions occur naturally, and you draw a rather strange inference from it. "There is an obvious truth here that cries out for acknowledgment: if God exists, He is the most prolific abortionist of all" (38). You do not appear to understand that if God is the giver of life (and He is)—"He Himself gives to all life and breath and all things" (Acts 17:25)—He may also take that life away. Job said it best: "The LORD gave and the LORD has taken away. Blessed be the name of the LORD" (Job 1:21). We cannot take life away on our own authority precisely because we did not give it in the first place. God the Creator does not have to answer to man the creature. He does not have to fill out a police report down at the station every time someone dies of a heart attack.

Any Reason He Should?

Your next section asks the question, "Are Atheists Evil?" Your argument here rests upon a common misunderstanding of a standard Christian argument, and so I am grateful for the opportunity to sort this out. In short, the issue is not whether atheists are evil, but rather, given atheism, what possible definition can we find for evil. The argument is not one about personal character but rather about what the tenets of atheism logically entail.

But there is another wrinkle as well. The Christian position is not that atheists are sinners, but rather that *people* are sinners. Consequently, when *any* false ideology (atheistic or theistic) gets a hold of a collective group of people, we are bound to find an area where there are no brakes to restrain the natural sinful tendencies of the people involved. This will of course manifest itself in different ways according to the differences of the ideologies. It explains why nations that are formally atheistic are awful (and dangerous) places to live. But at the same time, we could all rattle off false theistic ideologies that turned the places they controlled into hellholes. This just means that men sin in different ways.

So all this happens because people are sinners—and the Christian faith accounts for the reality and influence of this sin. *Theistic* rulers of Israel put Jesus to death, and this is obviously something that Christians condemn. Theistic Christian societies in the medieval period exhibited murderous behavior toward Jews, and this too is something that any Christian with an open Bible would have to condemn. Mao murdered his millions in the grip of his atheistic ideology, and we stand against that as well. It is not that theistic totalitarians are okay with us and atheistic totalitarianism is not. We reject it *all* because God hates it all and will bring it into judgment at the last day. He is not going to wave through the pearly gates all the murderous thugs who did their evil in His name. Quite the reverse.

A quick comment on your comparisons of advanced societies (as the "least religious societies on earth") to the third worlders (bringing up the rear) which you identify as "unwaveringly religious." What you left out of that evaluation is what worldview was predominant in all the advanced countries you mention when they *first* attained that advanced position. All of the nations you mentioned (with the exception of Japan) were Christian at the time of their ascendancy. Not only so, but many of the nations you mention, having abandoned their Christian heritage, arc also on their last legs. Europe, the remains of old Christendom, has about twenty years left before they go under the Islamic flood. In short, you have given us a picture of a cluster of prodigal sons, laughing in a tavern while spending their fathers' money and buying drinks for the house. But there is a difference between what it takes to make money and what it takes to spend it. The nations you mention became prosperous when they were under the strong influence of the Christian faith. They have abandoned that faith for the most part, and we shall now see how they will do. The checks are already starting to bounce.

Having made that point, let's return to the center of your argument. "If you are right to believe that religious faith offers the only real basis for morality, then atheists should be less moral than believers" (38–39). Again, the

LETTER FROM A CHRISTIAN CITIZEN

argument is not about the actual behavior of people. The argument is about what the actual behavior of people would be if they were logically consistent. As mentioned above, collective atheism tends toward that logical consistency, which is why I would oppose atheistic societies. But there is no reason to oppose, in the same way, an individual atheist who cannot see the logical outworkings of his own position. I am willing to cheerfully grant that there are many atheists that I would be happy to have live next door to me. I would be happy to ask them to watch my house while I was on vacation. I would not be compelled to think that as soon as we pulled around the corner, his atheism would compel him to run over and burn my house down.

Think of it this way. Let us suppose we have two men of atrocious character—they have both raped and murdered repeatedly and have expressed their contempt for the dignity of mankind in many other secret ways as well. They are both of them a piece of work, but one is a convinced atheist and the other is (in his intellectual commitments anyway) a Christian and a member of a Christian church. Now suppose further that because these two men are very clever, or because they were lucky enough to have incompetent cops assigned to their cases, or for whatever other reason, they both got away with their crimes, with no suspicion falling on either one of them. They both reached eighty years of age as respected members of their communities. Both of them successfully managed to live a double life. They have both come to their death beds, their crimes hidden and their intellectual commitments intact. One is still an atheist and the other still a Christian.

The first thinks to himself, "I made it through the obstacle course. I did whatever I wanted to do. I am about to die, and I will *never* have to answer for anything that I ever did." The second man is increasingly troubled in his conscience because "I got away with everything *here*, but I am going to a place where everything will be made manifest and judged." The former believes that he will not be judged for any of his crimes, and the second man believes that he will be judged for all of them. Now, given your atheism, which man is correct? This reveals that the wicked Christian lived an inconsistent life, while the wicked atheist lived a consistent life. His consistent lifestyle is not binding on you personally, but you are in no position to reject it for *him*.

Now my question is *not* "Are you a horrible criminal like the first man?" The question is not whether or not you as an atheist are promoting the same criminal choices that this other atheist made. I am not like the Christian in this illustration, and there is no reason why you have to be like that atheist.

My question is simply this: having made those choices and congratulating himself on his death bed, where is he wrong in his reasoning? I am not saying that his reasons provide a good rationale for you to go live that way—you obviously don't want to. But he *did* want to and what in your thinking can persuade him to think differently? And the use of this phrase "want to" identifies where the problem is. Given atheism, morality reduces to personal preferences. You don't need to protest that you don't share *those* preferences. I grant it. But the man in my illustration doesn't share yours either. Any reason he should?

God's Fast Ball, High and Inside

The first part of your next section ("Who Puts the Good in the 'Good Book'?) is actually quite strong. You begin by pointing out that the point of truth is not our own personal convenience. "Even if atheism led straight to moral chaos, this would not suggest that the doctrine of Christianity is true" (46). In other words, the "facts of the case" never check with us first to see if "them being true" will put us out in any way. The square of the hypotenuse is what it is quite apart from me having indigestion over it. Two apples added to two apples will result in four apples however stern my letter to the editor might be. In short, truth is what it is. And thus far we for the most part agree.

But this is a two-edged point. I grant your central point about atheism—the fact that a truth leading straight to moral chaos does not make an opposing position true. But, as I said, this sentiment cuts both ways. The fact is that Christianity might lead straight to moral chaos, as *you* define it (after all, Christ came to turn father against son, and daughter against mother, and brought a sword instead of peace), and yet not be false.

The one word you use in the quote above that I might take issue with is the word *suggest*. If that word were *prove*, I would agree, but *suggest* is a good bit milder. If atheism leads to moral chaos, then would it not be wise to at least *check* some of the alternatives? Jesus taught this principle with regard to those who were considering what it meant to be His disciple, what it meant to follow Him. He told us to count the cost, and this means that there will be short-term costs to count. Hard consequences *suggest* that we ought to check our calculations more than once.

The difference between us is that the Christian knows that there will be short-term chaos, but also knows that God has it under control, and that all things work together for good for those who love God and are the called according to His purpose (Romans 8:28). The atheist who runs into moral chaos has arrived at his final home, given the truth of his premises. Nevertheless, we can agree on this at least—the truth is independent of our wishes and desires.

In the first part of this section, you rightly admonish liberal and moderate Christians for wanting to have it both ways. "God remains an absolute mystery, a mere source of consolation that is compatible with the most desolating evil" (48). You say that "liberal theology must stand revealed for what it is: the sheerest of mortal pretenses. The theology of wrath has far more intellectual merit" (48). In other words, the world is a screwed up place, and *if* there is a God over it, then He cannot *just* be a comforter. The evil that exists in this world is here because God wills it, as everyone who believes in God must acknowledge at some level. He either wills it directly by His decrees (as I and my fellow Calvinists would say), or He wills it by allowing it to happen when He has the power to stop it (as other Christians hold). If some believers want to get away from this argument by appealing to something like "free will," this only explains *why* God wills it. It does not alter, in the slightest, the *fact* that God willed it. So we agree here as well.

You used the example of the great Asian tsunami. We agree that, if there is a God, He did not find out about this disaster from CNN.

He governs the earth, and this was something that happened on His watch. "If disaster befalls a city," the prophet Amos said, "have not I, the Lord, done it?" (Amos 3:6). And so when you say that a "theology of wrath" has far more "intellectual merit," I agree. It is consistent with the facts. Those who are nicknamed Calvinists do not have any unique problems with the "problem of evil." They just get more attention than other Christians on this point because they are willing to speak directly into the microphone. "Yes. God did this thing. And do you think that those on whom the tower fell were greater sinners? Unless you repent you will all likewise perish" (Luke 13:5).

But it is not only wrath. This wrath is something that God invites us to flee *from*. And the only way to flee from the wrath of God is to flee *to* the wrath of God as exhibited on the cross where Jesus suffered, bled, and died. But God does tell us to flee from the wrath to come, which is only done through repentance and faith in Jesus Christ. He does not tell us to flee from the doctrine of wrath in sophisticated embarrassment.

But I want to take this a step further. You are exactly right that *all* Christians, if they are to be intellectually honest, must acknowledge that God is the ultimate governor of earthquakes, tsunamis, hurricanes, genocides, and wars. This creates the "problem of evil" for us. How can a God who is infinitely just, kind, merciful, and loving (which we Christians also affirm) be the same one who unleashes these terrible "acts of God"? It is a good question, but it is one that can only be answered by embracing the problem. We solve the problem of evil by kissing the rod and the hand that wields it.

This sounds outrageous to you, I know, but it is the only way to genuinely deal with the problem of evil. It is either "the problem of evil," which the Christian has, or "Evil? No problem!," which the atheist has. Consider the tsunami from *your* premises. You spoke of the day "one hundred thousand children were simultaneously torn from their mother's arms and casually drowned" (48). Now I can only understand you being indignant with God over this if He is really *there*. But what if He is *not* there? What follows then? This event had no more ultimate significance than a solar flare or a virus going extinct or a desolate asteroid colliding with another asteroid or the gradual loss of Alabama to kudzu or me scratching my head just now. These are just atoms banging around. This is what they do.

It is very clear from how you write that you do not believe that God is there, and you are also very angry with Him for not being there. Many of these people who were drowned were no doubt praying before they died. You throw that fact at us believers (which you can do, because, believing in God, we do have a problem of evil). But if we throw it back to you, what must *you* say about the tsunami and its effects? It was a natural event driven by natural causes and has to be seen as an integral part of the natural order of things. There was absolutely *nothing* wrong with it. These things happen. Take the words of appalling comfort that John Lennon wrote for us.

> *Imagine there's no Heaven*
> *It's easy if you try*
> *No hell below us*
> *Above us only sky*
> *Imagine all the people*
> *Living for today*

But they are not living for today, not any more. Their bloated bodies are "dragged from the sea" (48). When their bodies are lined up on the beach, you want to rage, but there is no object for your anger. There is no wall to punch. Because above you *and them* is "only sky." You want to rail against God, but He is not there. *But that means He didn't do it.* So who did? There is no who. Only sky above us and only dirt below. In short, you have no right to exhibit the slightest bit of indignation over "the neglect" that is being shown to these particular end products of mindless evolution. There is no neglect. Nature eats her own and will do so until every last sun has gone out. Deal with it.

You may want to turn this around and pretend that I say these things because I am calloused. Not a bit of it. I am a Christian and I know that death and evil and disasters are all enemies. We are not without natural affection. Pure religion visits widows and orphans in their affliction (James 1:27). True religion is surprised at the last day to discover that God remembers all the acts of kindness done, down to the last drink of cold water. (Matt. 25:34–40). True religion will ask, "Lord, when did we do these things for you?" And He will *reply*. As Francis Schaeffer memorably put it, "He is there, and He is not silent."

When we look at the horrific things that happen in this world, there really are only two options: either these things have a larger purpose or they do not. If they do, then they will tie into that larger purpose at some point under the mastery of God, and all manner of things shall be well. This is the deeply comedic vision for the world that the Christian faith offers and which Peter Leithart describes so well in his recent book *Deep Comedy*.[4] But if they have no larger purpose, then there is nothing wrong with them *now* just the way they are. If the two of us were looking at a news report of the latest atrocity, I would say that at some point in the future, in some fundamental way, that will be *put right*. You want to say, as an atheist, that it will not ever be put right. But you refuse, for some reason, to take the next logical step and admit that there is therefore nothing wrong with it now. I will say more about this inconsistency in a future section.

One more thing. You say, "You are using your own moral intuitions to authenticate the wisdom of the Bible—and then, in the next moment, you assert that we human beings cannot possibly rely upon our own intuitions to rightly guide us in the world; rather, we must depend upon the prescriptions of the Bible. You are using your own moral intuitions to decide that the Bible is the appropriate guarantor of your moral intuitions. Your own intuitions are still primary, and your reasoning is circular. *We* decide what is good in the Good Book" (49). This criticism would apply to those who come to the Bible to cherry pick their inspirational verses. But I do not see how it applies to those who are willing to accept the Bible as it comes and who are willing to learn how to submit to the discipline of thinking scripturally across the board. Lots of people *do* project their middle class values onto the Bible and skate right over the embarrassing parts. But how would you deal with biblical absolutists who are willing to take the Bible as God's fast ball, high and inside? I don't see how your critique would apply at all to those of us in that category.

For example, immediately after this point, you cite Deuteronomy 22:13–21 and say, "If we are civilized, we will reject this as the vilest lunacy imaginable" (50). I have argued from that passage before in my book on biblical courtship[5], and I don't find this law of God's even a little bit shameful. I wouldn't dream of calling it "vile lunacy." So, what do you mean by "civilized"? Multiple questions arise. What does it mean to be civilized? Is it bad to be uncivilized? What are the standards of civilization, and who sets them? Why are those standards binding? Were the Aztecs civilized? How do civilizations arise? Did any great civilizations ever arise by having a higher view of Deuteronomy than you currently do?

Kerosene the Whole Ant Hill

You then continue a point in your next section—with variations—that we have already discussed. But the more you press this point, the clearer the issues become. I am happy to go over this again because your additional comments set the problem up nicely.

I want to begin by noting the particular problem of this section first. You have already chastised Christian believers over the problem of evil, and I have responded at that level. But here you present your atheism as a clear-sighted willingness to follow the argument all the way to the end, whatever the cost. But I actually have to admonish you here—you do nothing of the kind. Yours is *not* an atheism which rejects God and accepts all the consequences of that rejection regardless of how hard those consequences may be. Having rejected God, you remain a sentimentalist with your sentiments miraculously suspended in mid-air.

You pull out all the stops in presenting us with a particular instance of evil.

> *Somewhere in the world a man has abducted a little girl. Soon he will rape, torture, and kill her. If an atrocity of this kind is not occurring at precisely this moment, it will happen in a few hours, or days at most. . . . The same statistics also suggest that this girl's parents believe—as you believe—that an all-powerful and all-loving God is watching over them and their family. Are they right to believe this? Is it good that they*

believe this? No. The entirety of atheism
is contained in this response (50–51).

Well, actually, depending on what you mean, no, it isn't. You do not go on to say that it is a matter of indifference whether or not they believe this. You think that it is *bad* that the parents believe this. But what does *bad* mean? By what standard? I have already shown that, given your premises, you have no grounds for denouncing the perpetrator of this horrific crime. Still less do you have grounds for denouncing the parents for not believing that the death of their little girl was ultimately senseless—as *you* would have them believe.

And this is where your sentimentalism kicks in with a vengeance. "An atheist is a person who believes that the murder of a single little girl—even once in a million years—casts doubt upon the idea of a benevolent God" (52). This is not even close. Why do you halt between two opinions? Atheism not only casts doubt upon the idea of a benevolent God (which it certainly does), *but it also destroys the very concept of benevolence itself.* Benevolence is simply a chemical reaction that some organisms experience in their bone box. Other organisms (like the criminal organism that rapes and kills the little girl organism) don't have very much of it. But this is all just time and chance acting on matter. When you reject the triune God (in the name of benevolence!) I want to know what this all-authoritative benevolence actually is, on *your* accounting.

I do not believe that the indignation you display over these monstrosities is a sham. I believe that you actually feel this way. But then to pretend that these sentiments of yours are actually part of a courageous willingness to ask and answer the hard questions is a bit thick. There is no soundtrack to consistent atheism. No swelling violins in the background but rather stark, everlasting *silence*.

Many atheists *have* squarely faced the consequences of what they say they believe, but you do not even begin to approach this. And this is why your question to Christians is sad more than anything else. "Do you have the courage to admit the obvious?" (52). Oliver Wendell Holmes did. He knew what morality was, given the premises. Preferences with regard to morality were just that, *preferences*. Moral

LETTER FROM A CHRISTIAN CITIZEN

preferences are "more or less arbitrary."[6] Let that settle in your mind, without your fragments of atheistic sanctimony—emotional detritus left over from the previous Christian era. And let Holmes spell it out for you. "Do you like sugar in your coffee or don't you? . . . So as to truth."[7] Or try this out: Truth is "the majority view of the nation which can lick all others."[8] And rights are "what a given crowd will fight for."[9]

If the material universe is what you claim, then you need to embrace the ramifications of what you claim. The wiping out of a nation or a city does not have the significance that you are unsuccessfully trying to create for it. Holmes again: "I doubt if a shudder would go through the spheres if the whole ant heap were kerosened."[10] Your ideas are nothing but epiphenomena in that curious chemical vat of yours that we are pleased to call a brain. But let Holmes point out the comparative value of one part of your body over another. "I wonder if cosmically an idea is any more important than the bowels."[11] Now not even Holmes is fully consistent with his premises, because if that thought of his were correct, then all thoughts are on the same level as a bowel movement, and that would include this particular thought of *his*, which would give us full liberty to ignore him. But although Holmes pulls up short before tumbling into the abyss, he is certainly willing to affirm far more of what is necessarily entailed in his atheism than you are. He is well down the road; you are still in the driveway. You say,

> *Once you stop swaddling the reality of the world's suffering in religious fantasies, you will feel in your bones just how precious life is—and, indeed, how unfortunate it is that millions of human beings suffer the most harrowing abridgements of their happiness for no good reason at all (54).*

There have been many clear-sighted atheists who have preceded you who have felt nothing of the kind in their bones. And they can explain to you clearly why, if there is nothing above us but sky, certain things follow. Your sentimental atheism is a hodge-podge of Christian leftovers.

You ask, "What was God doing while Katrina laid waste to their city?" (52). Well, to give the biblical answer, during Katrina, *God* was laying waste to the city. This is something even insurance companies know; it was an act of God. He is not an absentee deity; scriptural Christians do not feel in the least bit apologetic about how God governs the world. What He did to New Orleans was holy, righteous, just and good. Some of it may have been an obvious chastisement for those who would build a major city below sea level in hurricane country and then attempt to govern it through corruption and vice.

Some of God's goodness was apparent on the face of it at the time, and some of the righteousness behind His action will not be apparent until the Last Day. But there is no blemish at all in God's ways with man. We believe by faith that God draws straight with crooked lines. You are free to reject this, as you clearly have. But when you reject it, you must acknowledge that you have *also* lost the very concept of a crooked line. And it follows that you must stop being indignant about these non-existent crooked lines.

Unaware of all this, you state the problem of evil in its classic form.

> *"This is the age-old problem of theodicy, of course, and we should consider it solved. If God exists, either He can do nothing to stop the most egregious calamities, or He does not care to. God, therefore, is either impotent or evil"* (55).

Yes, this is the problem of evil, and it is the question that every Christian theist must answer. Since the idea of divine impotence in effect un-gods God, not many of us have taken this route. But in this effeminate age, some professing Christians are now trying it, and they call their explanation the "openness of God." God troubleshoots as we go, but He actually does not do it very well. In this view, God reacts to disasters as they happen, but His reflexes are pretty poor. He runs after disasters, wringing His hands. In this view, God is a lot like FEMA—unprepared, incompetent, disorganized, and two weeks late.

The other option is that God does not want to stop the evil just now. If He wanted to stop it, He would have. This is exactly right. But we believe, beyond just this raw statement, that God has *glorious* reasons for this unwillingness to intervene. Those glorious reasons will be made manifest on the day when every mouth will be stopped, and every tongue confesses that all His actions throughout all history were good and true. Until that day, we take it on faith.

You say that you cannot accept this. You don't have that faith. Fair enough. But you must know that this means that you *also* do not have the faith to believe that there are such things as benevolence, kindness, mercy, and love. Either mercy is genuine and real, and the tension along with the existence of genuine evil requires faith in the triune God of the Bible; or we reject that tension—and the reality of mercy and evil along with it. What you call mercy is nothing more than what happens when you pour vinegar into the baking soda. When we look at a fourth grader's science fair project, it does not occur to us to pronounce that his paper mache volcano is speaking profound truths or exhibiting great philanthropy. If this is what you want to claim, then go right ahead. And if you do, we won't listen because the next book you write (just like the previous ones) is just the smoke from the chemical reaction down in the hole. But if you don't want to claim it, then you need to drop everything and spend some time searching for your god. For in that case nothing would be more apparent than the fact that you *have* one and you are no atheist at all.

"It is terrible that we all die and lose everything we love; it is doubly terrible that so many human beings suffer needlessly while alive" (56–57). And this is my point. In your view, all suffering is (by definition) senseless. It is not immediately needless, given the evolutionary struggle that you say is occurring, but in the larger view of things, it is meaningless. And since evolution is not anything that anybody actually requested, I guess it is needless at that level also. The Holocaust is on the same level as boys pouring kerosene in the ant hill, just for fun and just because they can. The Christian is the one saying that all this will eventually be put right. You are the one saying it *cannot* be put right and by unacknowledged implication, that there is nothing wrong with it now.

Ironically, after unwittingly marshalling all these inconsistencies, you then say that "criticism of religious faith [is] a moral and intellectual necessity" (57). All right, then, criticize away. Assemble the ants to complain about the boulder that rolled down the hill and destroyed their prosperous city. Circulate a petition. File that indignant petition with the authorities . . . wait. There are no authorities. Above the outraged ants, only sky. Nobody is in charge of this. Nobody did it. Stuff just happens.

All Over Tarnation

In your next section, "The Power of Prophecy," we move from the "great" questions like the problem of evil to some particular and specific questions you raise about the Bible.

You say that Christians argue that "many of the ideas recounted in the New Testament confirm Old Testament prophecy" (57). A better way of putting it is that we believe many of the predictions made in the Old Testament of the coming Messiah were fulfilled in the New, but your expression of it is certainly fair enough. But you then go on to claim that it would be really easy to rig this kind of fulfillment. "Wouldn't it have been within the power of any mortal to write a book that confirms the predictions of a previous book?" (57) Well, in the abstract that would be very easy to do. But you are leaving out of your reckoning the fact that the Christian faith was first preached and established in the face of stiff opposition. You are not the first debunker that the Christian faith has ever encountered. This means that when the disciples wrote their gospel accounts of Christ's life, they were doing so in a hostile environment in which any attempt to be cute with the known facts would be immediately turned against them. It is in this setting that we should take note of the prophecies of Christ's birthplace in Bethlehem (a hard event to stage), the betrayal price that Judas took, the details of Christ's passion, and, most important, the predictions of His resurrection. Coming back from the dead after three days in the tomb is notoriously hard to rig. As the apostle Paul once put it, "These things were not done in a corner" (Acts 26:26). Everybody was watching what was happening, friend and foe alike. After-the-fact prophecy-fulfillment is not hard in a vacuum, but it would have been hard in the circumstances in which the Christian faith first took root.

Some of your other objections do not go very deep, and so I don't think I need to spend a lot of time with them. For example, you point to the prophecy in Isaiah about a virgin conceiving and giving birth to a son who will be named "God with us," and you rightly note that the Hebrew word *alma* means virgin *or* young woman. This is quite correct. Isaiah is giving a double prophecy here—a young woman in his day would conceive (as a sign to Ahaz) and a virgin would conceive a child sometime in the future. This is a double prophecy which is allowed for in the Hebrew. But we can see that something is up in the Greek translation of this passage in the Septuagint. This translation was done centuries *after* Isaiah and long *before* the advent of Christ. No Christians had anything to do with it, and these Old-Testament-era Jews translated *alma* into Greek as *parthenos*, which can *only* mean virgin. The expectation of the Jews prior to Christ included an expectation of a virgin birth.

So this is how I would answer your assertion that *virgin* was a Christian mistranslation. "It seems all but certain that the dogma of the virgin birth, and much of the Christian world's resulting anxiety about sex, was a product of a mistranslation from the Hebrew" (58). As to your assertion that Christians have a deep-seated anxiety over sex, I would counter by suggesting that for *real* sexual angst, you would have to try someplace like Manhattan. Looking around at churches here in Idaho and judging from all the kids there, it would seem to me that a bunch of Christians didn't get the memo.

You also bring up a problem with how the biblical writers arranged their footnotes, calling this an error of "scholarship." "And the evangelists made other errors of scholarship. Matthew 27:9–10, for instance, claims to fulfill a saying that it attributes to Jeremiah. The saying actually appears in Zechariah 11:12–13" (58). But what you fail to take into account here is the fact that it was a custom among the Jews, when referring to *two* sources, to have the attribution go to the major prophet, which in this case was Jeremiah. Jeremiah does give a prophecy that in Israel's future fields will be bought for silver (Jer. 32:9), and Zechariah's prophecy is more specific, mentioning the amount that Judas would receive (Zech. 11:12–13). Matthew is referring to both, quotes one, and gives the credit, according to their custom, to the major prophet. Your objection here actually amounts to saying that Matthew should have followed the *Chicago Manual of Style*. But it would be just as valid for Matthew to claim that you had cited a source incorrectly because you wrote *Ibid* in one of your footnotes. "I looked and looked," Matthew said, "and there is no book in the whole library called *Ibid*."

On another front, you complain that the Bible doesn't really treat some of the subjects you would have preferred. "A book written by an omniscient being could contain a chapter on mathematics that, after two thousand years of continuous use, would still be the richest source of mathematical insight humanity has ever known. Instead, the Bible contains no formal discussion of mathematics and some obvious mathematical errors . . ." (60). Well, the first part of this is right, in a weird kind of way. But a complaint of this nature amounts to an unwillingness to let God be God and tell us what He would like us to know and to do so in a way that reveals what *He* believes to be important. We have no mathematical books in the Bible—to take an extreme example of what I am saying here—for the same reason that God did not include the perfect *Star Trek* novella in there. Mathematics as a subject is just fine, and God thought it was cool enough to embed it in everything He made for us to discover, but it is not nearly as important in the communication of divine truth as poetry is. We can tell this by looking at how God actually speaks to us. Your preference for mathematics over poetry evidences a marked Hellenistic bias over the Hebraic mind. But there is no *a priori* reason why we should think that mathematics is capable of doing for us what the Scriptures (as they actually are) do for us.

But even though mathematics does not warrant a separate book of its own in the Bible, this is no reason for asserting that Scripture contains mathematical errors. As an example of one of the "obvious mathematical errors" (1 Kings 7:23–26 and 2 Chronicles 4:2–5), which you say state that "the ratio of the circumference of a circle to its diameter" is 3 to 1. This, you say, is "not impressive" (61). But these passages say nothing of the kind. The Scriptures are not telling us the value of *pi*. They are not talking about "a circle" in the abstract. They are talking about the bronze laver or "sea" that Solomon had ordered to be cast. This is a measurement of an actual bronze laver in the real world, and in that world, unlike the pristine world of Euclid, the line of the circumference has an actual *thickness*. The laver was not made out of a paper-thin sheet of bronze.

You are suggesting that if Euclid had been able to visit Solomon for a little geometry workshop, Solomon would have been scratching his head over Euclid's insistence that Solomon not be allowed to build a laver with a circumference of 30 cubits and a diameter of 10 cubits.

"But I want to," Solomon would say.

"Well, you can't," Euclid fired back.

"What shall I do with the one we already have?"

"I'm sorry, you don't have one. It's not possible," Euclid said.

"What's not possible," Solomon said, "is a laver made out of mathematical points. We tried that. It leaked all over tarnation."

What Color Are Your Arguments?

Your next section, "The Clash of Science and Religion," begins by taking issue with the National Academy of Sciences. Among other things, that august academy said, "Science can say nothing about the supernatural. Whether God exists or not is a question about which science is neutral" (63). You took issue with this because, as you put it, "The truth, however, is that the conflict between religion and science is unavoidable" (63).

Now I need to say at the outset that I *agree* with you that there is a necessary clash between "neutral" science and religion. This is because I believe that there is no such thing as neutrality anywhere. If there is a triune God, and if Jesus Christ is His only-begotten Son, then this divine being is not confined in anything as tiny as the "supernatural." Jesus Christ is Lord of all or He is not Lord at all. This means that He is the Lord of all science. We both reject the truce offered by the National Academy of Sciences, but for different reasons. I reject it because I believe the lordship of Christ swallows up so-called scientific neutrality. You reject it because, in effect, what you will accept as reasonable evidence swallows up all claims to truth that fall outside the definitions you have set.

But having said this, how you go about defining science is truly curious. You say, "The core of science is not controlled experiment or mathematical modeling; it is intellectual honesty" (64). You do this to allow for historical claims to be lumped under science—the example you used is the fact that the Japanese bombed Pearl Harbor in 1941. Anything that is intellectually honest is science; anything that is intellectually dishonest is not. Okay. Now who is in charge of determining this? The National Academy of Intellectual Honesty?

You say something similar here:

> *"It is time we acknowledged a basic feature of human discourse: when considering the truth of a proposition, one is either engaged in an honest appraisal of the evidence and logical arguments, or one isn't. Religion is the one area of our lives where people imagine that some other standard of intellectual integrity applies"* (64–65).

Now you have already allowed that historical claims are, in principle, scientific claims, provided they are made by men and women who are intellectually honest. So what do you do with the claim that Jesus rose from the dead? Christians claim that this happened in history, not in a transcendent supernatural realm. We claim it took place in Jerusalem. According to Scripture, and according the basic Christian confession of the Creed, it occurred "under Pontius Pilate." Now this is a historical claim, straight up the middle, pure and simple. You said, in the quote above, that intellectual honesty will engage in "an honest appraisal of the evidence." What does this look like when we Christians are making our scientific claim (according to your unique definition) about the raising of Jesus from the dead? Do you go check the empty tomb? Is that part of an honest appraisal of the evidence? Or do you have an *a priori* assumption that such a thing cannot happen because it has never happened before? And because of that assumption do you refuse to look at the evidence? Who is being intellectually honest in such a circumstance—the person who runs to the tomb, like Peter, or the one who doesn't?

We *understand* the person who doesn't bother even to check a story like this, but of course, we would understand him equally well if a couple of goofball time-travelers from the 21st century showed up in first-century Palestine with a DVD and a plasma television set (and a portable generator). They set up a little theater on the south side of the city and invite everyone to come see *Pride and Prejudice* (with subtitles in Aramaic). Now is

the person who refuses to come look at this
fraud (or display of demonism, take your
choice) being scientific or not? According to
your new definition of science, anyone who
refused to check out these things known to
him to be thundering impossibilities (but
which are known to *us* to be common and
everyday sorts of things) is being intellectually
dishonest. But this seems a bit harsh. After
all, imagine trying to explain (to someone
like George Washington) your handheld
calculator, your laptop, the Internet, your
cell phone, nuclear reactors, your iPod, and
your pickup truck. But if enough people that
he trusted said, "Come, *see* . . .," he might
be persuaded to come and see. And what
if he saw? Suppose you are Washington's
hard-bitten cynical friend who refused to
go with him. And when he came back, you
still refused to believe him because of your *a
priori* assumptions about what was and was
not possible? Is that science?

You say, "The conflict between science and
religion is reducible to a simple fact of human
cognition and discourse: either a person has
good reasons for what he believes or he does

not" (66–67). Did Peter, having seen the risen Lord, have good reason for believing in the resurrection? You would say that *if* he did see Him, then he would have good reason, but he didn't see him because he *couldn't* have seen him. But you are saying this on the basis of an *a priori* assumption about the universe, and not on the basis of how we normally go about establishing historical claims, which is by means of weighing eye-witness accounts. If you had an *a priori* assumption that you lived in a universe in which Japanese attacks on Pearl Harbor were an impossibility, well then, when the witnesses start showing up with their crazy stories, you know just what to do.

You then say something else that is curious. "Everyone recognizes that to rely upon 'faith' to decide specific questions of historical fact is ridiculous" (67). Well, this is strange. Peter and James and John didn't rely on faith to determine that Jesus rose. They relied on their eyes and hands. And Thomas was the most empirical of them all. He wouldn't believe unless he actually saw and touched the risen Jesus. There it is—real-life science in action and in the Bible! They confirmed that He rose the same way they confirmed everything else that happened in their lives. And for those of us who did *not* see the risen Jesus, we rely on their eyewitness testimony. I did not see the Lord rise, the battle of Waterloo, the great fire of London, or George Washington crossing the Delaware. But I believe that all of them happened, and I do so for the same exact reason. I find the eyewitness testimony that has come down to us concerning these events to be credible. Why am I intellectually dishonest for believing the first item on this list, but not for believing the remaining three? You would say it is because a resurrection from the dead is a miracle, and miracles don't happen. But this is your materialist faith kicking in again. This is a mere assumption of yours.

And speaking of your materialist *faith*, here is something else that you say. "It is time that we admitted that faith is nothing more than the license religious people give one another to keep believing when reasons fail" (67). It is clear from what we have discussed that you have faith also—faith that the universe is a closed system and that something like a resurrection is inconceivable. But this is not something you discovered by looking into a microscope. It is a philosophical axiom of yours—it is an article of *faith*. And, as we have just learned, faith is nothing more than "the license that atheists give one another to keep on not believing when reasons press in on them."

You say: "Religion is the one area of our discourse where it is considered noble to pretend to be certain about things no human being could possibly be certain about" (67). You are certain that Peter did not see Jesus when He rose from the dead. But this certainty of yours arises from your convictions about the nature of the universe, and not because you were in the room with Peter when he started talking to his invisible friend. Isn't that correct?

One last thing. The closed system that makes up your universe *is* impervious to any evidence to the contrary. Once you grant that the world works this way, anyone who comes bustling up to you with stories about men who came back from the dead is a *prima facie* nutjob. Simple. But you need to look at your closed-system-universe again and look more closely at the price tag this time. Not only is this vast concourse of atoms spared the spectacle of a Jewish carpenter coming back from the grave, it is also spared *all* forms of immaterial realities. This would include, unfortunately, your arguments and thoughts. They are as immaterial as Farley's ghost. Show me your arguments for atheism under a microscope. Then I will think about believing them. What color at they? How much do they weigh? *What* are they made of?

You Tell Me That It's Evolution; Well, You Know . . .

Of course, we were bound to get to the subject of evolution sooner or later. And this is unlikely to be the place where we both discover that we are "actually saying the same thing really." You think that creationists are bereft of any intellectual dignity whatever, and I agree with Malcolm Muggeridge that in retrospect evolution will be seen to have been one of the great jokes of history. Well, if your cavalry and ours are going to collide, we might as well do it at full gallop.

You maintain that evolution is a nailed-down fact, beyond all questioning. If someone does raise questions, this just demonstrates that he is a lunatic, and not that the question should have been raised. You say, in multiple ways, that evolution is "beyond all questioning." Well, here come some questions anyway.

> *All complex life on earth has developed from simpler life-forms over billions of years. This is a fact that no longer admits of intelligent dispute (68).*

I know that I am arguing with someone whose position is "what my net don't catch ain't fish," and that anyone who postulates that fish can be small enough to fit through a hole two inches square is an idiot. But here goes anyway. You begin by saying that the common use of the word *theory* does not detract from your case.

> *Theories make predictions and can, in principle, be tested. The phrase 'the theory of evolution' does not in the least suggest that evolution is not a fact (69).*

Your argument is that a theory is just a larger web of facts. A datum is a fact; a scientific theory is a cluster of facts with no loss of facticity involved. Thus, for you, the theory of evolution is as factually settled as the germ theory of disease is.

So what should we call a "theory" that can still be falsified? Is relativity theory a fact? Will physicists 500 years from now hold to the same identical theory . . . because it is an undisputed assemblage of *facts*? Thomas Kuhn was not talking about the theory of evolution in his book *The Structure of Scientific Revolutions*, but his description of how one paradigm passes from the stage and is replaced by another is an uncanny description of what is happening today to your beloved theory of evolution.[12] One of the tell-tale signs of trouble for a theory or a paradigm is when its defenders resort to name-calling in lieu of argument and obstinately defend an ossified orthodoxy instead of answering reasonable questions. And this is why science advances, as Max Planck observed, funeral by funeral.

In passing, you try to deal with all the creationists who have somehow obtained advanced degrees in the hard sciences. "A handful of Christians appear to have done this;

some have even obtained their degrees from reputable universities" (69). The first part of this is not quite accurate—a "handful"? My brother is one of these interlopers, and I can assure you that your minimized head counts reveal more than a little wishful thinking. You then deal with the problem with some hand-waving sleight of definition. "While such people are technically 'scientists,' they are not behaving like scientists" (70). And why not? Well, they apparently disagree with *you*. Your field is philosophy, and what you are doing here amounts to saying that anyone who is a Kantian, for example, can't be a *real* philosopher. This is a sure indicator that an established position is in real trouble. Never, *ever*, engage. Just simply assert.

> *We know that all complex organisms on earth, including ourselves, evolved from earlier organisms over the course of billions of years. The evidence for this is utterly overwhelming (70).*

Okay, could we who are numbered with the underwhelmed see some the evidence? Can we talk about it? Will questions be allowed, or is this a "just have faith, my son" sort of religion? But then, even in the midst of your assertions, you give the game away.

> *There is no question that the diverse life we see around us is the expression of a genetic code written in the molecule DNA, that DNA undergoes chance mutations, and that some mutations increase an organism's odds of surviving and reproducing in a given environment (70–71).*

You get back on your evolutionary message in the second part of this quotation— "chance mutations" and "increase odds." But look what you let slip in the first part. "There is no question that the diverse life we see around us is the expression of *a genetic code written.*" Exactly so—codes are *written.* A strand of DNA is a vast library. Scientists who have their satellite dishes pointed toward the sky in the hope of hearing from intelligent life out there know how to distinguish incoming messages from background noise. Otherwise, there would be no point. We know what information looks like, and we know what kind of source it comes from. This is because information is not made out of matter—rather it is matter that is organized in a particular way. If a scientist studying static from solar flare activity was to discover that all his printouts kept repeating the St. Crispin's Day speech from *Henry V*, his conclusion would *not* be that "given infinity and randomness, this was bound to happen sooner or later." And one strand of DNA is not just one speech from Shakespeare—it is the whole library.

But you persist in clinging to what you were taught by the priests in your youth.

There is no question that human beings evolved from nonhuman ancestors. We know, from genetic evidence, that we share an ancestor with apes and monkeys, and that this ancestor in turn shared an ancestor with the bats and the flying lemurs (71).

No question. No question. No *question*. Just keep saying that. But while we are on the subject, why did we decide to get rid of our uncanny sonar abilities? And since we are nothing but souped-up lemurs, let me raise (*again*) the question of the trustworthiness of our thought processes. Let us assume that evolution is not done with us, and we keep on advancing through the fog. When we have evolved for ten million more years, and our distant descendants look back on us, will they think of our current cogitations and philosophies as barely distinguishable from lemur-thought? If not, then how is that evolution? If so, why should we trust *anything* that we are currently thinking?

You felt, obviously, the need to take on the critics of evolution who are found in the Intelligent Design movement. But, not surprisingly, you are dismissive, and you do not really take them on at all. According to you, ID is "nothing more than a program of political and religious advocacy masquerading as science" (72).

The way you try to engage with them, however, shows that you are grossly unacquainted with the literature. "The argument runs more or less like this:

everything that exists has a cause" (72). You are trying to summarize the arguments of the contemporary ID movement, and what you actually do is haul out an argument from the medieval theologian Thomas Aquinas. But the characteristic arguments of ID involve concepts like information theory and irreducible complexity. From *your* summary, it is pretty clear that you have not read any of the ID stuff. Why are you going into print on it? This nagging suspicion is clinched with this observation of yours.

> *Even if we accepted that the universe*
> *simply had to be designed by a designer,*
> *this would not suggest that this designer*
> *is the biblical God or that He approves*
> *of Christianity (73).*

Here you are trying to argue against ID by employing one of the arguments *that they themselves make.* ID advocates will tell you that their arguments do not prove the existence of God and are not intended to. That is one of the problems that I as a Christian have with the ID movement. I really appreciate the demolition job they are doing on Darwin, but I think they should drive their truck a lot further down the road and then unload the whole thing. A variation of the "infinite regress" (73) argument that you make is an argument that I have presented before to a friend of mine in the ID movement. But the reason I bring this up is that what this proves is that you are interacting with a movement and you have not taken the trouble to read (or at least remember) some of their basic arguments. Before you set up shop to dismiss the ID arguments, you should at least ascertain what they are.

Just one more point, and then I am done. You say: "The biologist J.B.S. Haldane is reported to have said that, if there is a God, He has 'an inordinate fondness for beetles.' One would have hoped that an observation this devastating would have closed the book on creationism for all time" (75–76). There are, as you point out, over 350,000 *species* of beetles. But why this should count as an argument against the triune God of Scripture, I surely don't know. I am a die-hard creationist, and I think it is the coolest thing in the world that our God created that many different kinds of beetles. What this really means is the God of Scripture is not the tidy god of Plato that philosophers prefer to believe (or disbelieve) in. I am a *Christian*; I love it when our God misbehaves like this.

Let the Dialogue Begin!

Your next to last section is entitled "Religion, Violence, and the Future of Civilization," but it could just as easily be named after Richard Weaver's famous book, *Ideas Have Consequences*. As you say, "The truth is, it really matters what billions of human beings believe and why they believe it" (87). I actually agreed with a number of things you said in this section but was troubled by the fact that you are trying to build a solid house on such a shaky foundation.

For example, you begin by saying, "Unfortunately, there are many books that pretend to divine authorship, and they make incompatible claims about how we all must live" (79). Well, sure. I agree with that. The Koran and the Bible, to take just two examples, cannot both be the Word of God. But how is this observation an argument against the concept of divine revelation? If there are a million dollars just sitting there, and somewhere out there is a long-lost heir, it is in the highest degree likely that many will show up claiming to be that heir. Nobody counterfeits brown shopping bags, but they do counterfeit twenty-dollar bills. To argue from numerous false claimants to the conclusion that there must not be an inheritance is a dubious procedure. To argue that there is no such thing as the Federal Reserve because of a rise in counterfeiting is not a structurally sound argument. When you have rival claims about ultimate reality, one of the things that you must do is sort them out.

You point out that our culture has grown hyper-sensitive about religious issues. "Our fear of provoking religious hatred has rendered us unwilling to criticize ideas that are increasingly maladaptive and patently ridiculous" (80). This is a good observation, but this is something that your secularism has done for us and all in the interest of building up mutual toleration and group hugs for everyone. And so, I would ask you, point blank, are you having second thoughts about secular liberalism? Do you believe that we should have a line on the form that immigrants must fill out that asks them if they think Allah is the one true God, and whether Mohammed is his prophet?

You also observe, again rightly, that "religion raises the stakes of human conflict much higher than tribalism, racism, or politics ever can, as it is the only form of in-group/out-group thinking that casts the differences between people in terms of eternal rewards and punishments" (80). You say that "one of the enduring pathologies of human culture is the tendency to raise children to fear and demonize other human beings on the basis of religious faith" (80). You are talking here about people in one religion despising members of another religion—but the same thing could be said about people despising others for even having a religion at all. For example, I recently read a book in which the author wrote that people who believe in God are deranged. Okay, I'm trying to be a little cute here . . . the book was yours. "It is not at all clear how we should proceed in our dialogue with the Muslim world, but deluding ourselves with euphemisms is not the answer" (85). You go on to say that "most Muslims are *utterly deranged by their religious faith*" (85, emphasis yours). After this, you add, "It seems profoundly unlikely that we will heal the divisions in our world through interfaith dialogue" (86). Well, yeah. Especially *that* kind of interfaith dialogue where you keep referring to your opponent as "you idiot."

I believe that Islam is a false religion, and I believe that the people who adhere to it are deluded. I believe that they are objectively wrong, and that the Christian faith is objectively right. But I believe that Muslims are men and women created in the image of God, fallen in sin, and potential recipients of the offered gospel of forgiveness in Christ. It is one thing to say that we ought to move away from politically-correct euphemisms (which I agree with), and then to go on to say that everyone in the history of the world outside your little atheistic society is a raving psychopathic wackjob. "Let the dialogue begin!" Coming from you, it sounds a bit hollow.

You give a long list of animosities, and say, *rightly*, that they "are often the products of their religious identities" (81). But again, for Christians, this is beside the point. We don't believe that religion is the answer. We believe Christ is the answer. When you combine religion with sinners, what you get is religious sin. And when you combine serious religion with sinners, what you get is *serious* religious sin. All this does is confirm one of the basic tenets of the Christian faith, which is that the human race is all screwed up.

At a number of points in this section, you turn your critique on your fellow secularists, pointing out that they have been a little naive. "And yet, while the religious divisions in our world are self-evident, many people still imagine that religious conflict is always caused by a lack of education, by poverty, or by politics" (82). You go on to add that "jihadist violence is not merely a matter of education, poverty, or politics" (83). This is exactly right. The problem of sin cannot be removed by education, money, or getting a bill through Congress. But neither can it be solved by getting rid of religion. All that does is give you a *secular* religion of the kind currently on tap in North Korea. The problem is not found in abstract nouns—like religion, education, wealth, etc. Neither is the solution to be found there. The problem is in concrete persons. People are sinful, and they want to throw rocks at one another. Put them down in one place and the rocks they throw will be basalt; in another region they will throw granite rocks. But they will throw *something*. If we are to solve the problems you point out in this section, something must be done with the people. I hope to say something about this in my last section.

In the meantime, "Western secularists, liberals, and moderates have been very slow to understand this. The cause of their confusion is simple: they don't know what it is like to *really* believe in God" (83). But again, from a Christian perspective there is obviously no problem with really believing in God. The problem is really believing in God in such a way that the basic sin problem of the human heart remains untouched.

You point out that Europe is in grave danger of being overrun by Islam, and everyone agrees with you here. You say, "The birth rate among European Muslims is three times that of their non-Muslim neighbors" (83). You lament the fact that the only voices raised in warning against this problem are those of fascists. Actually, many Christians are talking about this problem also, but from your book it appears that joining with Christians to do something about this would be as detestable to you as joining with the fascists. But nevertheless, the problem isn't going away. "France will be a majority-Muslim country in twenty-five years—and that is if immigration were to stop tomorrow" (83–84).

And this leaves you with a real dilemma. You want to save the secular democracies of Europe. You want to do it without religion. But secularism, which has apparently taken to worshipping the condom, produces low birth rates and is consequently in mortal danger of being overrun within the next twenty years. Ideas *do* have consequences. And what does Darwin say about one population replacing another?

The Ultimate Story

I hope you have taken the time to read through this short response to your small book. Whether you have or not, I do not regret taking the time to compose this—your writings on this subject are certainly widespread, and this response has enabled me to speak, not only to you, but to anyone interested in the other side of the story.

In this last section, I want to do two things. The first is to address briefly some of the comments you made in your final conclusion. The second thing is to make a brief statement of the Christian faith in the context of our discussion.

In a previous section, I said that you were trying to function as a sentimental atheist. To echo the famous words of C.S. Lewis, you remove the organ and demand the function. You castrate and bid the gelding to be fruitful. This comes home with a vengeance in your conclusion where you talk about what you want the human race to do. "One of the greatest challenges facing civilization in the twenty-first century is for human beings to learn to speak about their deepest personal concerns—about ethics, spiritual experience, and the inevitability of human suffering—in ways that are not flagrantly irrational" (87). You write here as though our "deepest personal concerns" have value. As we make "ethical" choices, as we experience something "spiritual," and as we contemplate the horror of human "suffering," you write and say that we have to learn how to speak about these things. I put "scare quotation" marks around those three words because on your account I am one set of complex chemical reactions secreting something that I falsely believe to be arguments to another set of complex chemical reactions who falsely believes that he is reading them.

"We must find ways to invoke the power of ritual and to mark those transitions in every human life that demand profundity—birth, marriage, death—without lying to ourselves about the nature of reality" (88). You want life to have meaning, and you want it to have meaning without shrinking back from the intellectual demands of raw atheism. In short, you want to square the circle and you cannot do it. But you keep trying. "But any genuine exploration of ethics or the contemplative life demand the same standards of reasonableness and self-criticism that animate all intellectual discourse" (90). But if you apply reason and self-criticism to an atheistic examination of ethics, you should discover within ten minutes *that there aren't any*.

But you say we must speak about these things and you demand at the front end intellectual honesty. "We desperately need a public discourse that encourages critical thinking and intellectual honesty" (87). Well, here is the honest answer. You are a hodge-podge of neuron-firings looking into an abyss which you only *think* you understand. You don't really understand it because you are not thinking at all, but rather doing what chemicals always do under those conditions and at that temperature. Consequently you have no reason to believe that anything you think is true, *including* the idea that all your thoughts are chemical reactions. You present yourself as willing to embrace the stark realities, but when you talk about ethics, *spiritual* experience, and concern over suffering, you give the game away. That is not atheism, but rather residue from your culture's Christian past.

You still want to speak as though the arrival of Darwin and secular Enlightenment set us all free from some really bad stuff. "The truth is, some of your most cherished beliefs are as embarrassing as those that sent the last slave ship sailing to America as late as 1859 (the same year that Darwin published *The Origin of Species*)" (88). Your implication is clear. Before Darwin, slavery. After Darwin, sweetness and light. But you really need to take a close look at the racist implications of Darwinism, and how those implications were *understood* and applied in the eugenics movement leading up to the Holocaust. The recent book *From Darwin to Hitler* spells it out pretty plainly.[13] Of course, I expect you to protest that such linkage is an historical slander, and that I am misrepresenting Darwinism's link to racism. But the facts speak for themselves, and you have been insisting that we follow the argument wherever it leads. So here is the argument. Given the fact that human beings evolved from primates, as you asserted earlier, is there any *a priori* reason why a *consistent* evolutionist wouldn't cheerfully agree that one race of human beings could certainly be lower on the evolutionary tree than the others? Any reason why, when we get to *homo sapiens*, magic suddenly intervenes and equality appears? *You* might believe in this equality (for social reasons), but Darwin and the entirety of his early entourage certainly didn't. Those of us who believe that all human races are descended from Noah don't struggle with the same problem, because we are all *human* cousins.

While lamenting the violence that religion has brought into the world, your language toward believers sometimes verges on the violent. "Only then will the practice of raising our children to believe that they are Christian, Muslim, or Jewish be widely recognized as the ludicrous obscenity that it is" (88). "Ludicrous obscenity?" Is that child abuse? Do you think children should be forcibly removed from such homes? You allow that religion may have bestowed some sort of evolutionary advantage at some point in our history, but you do not throw this out as a compliment. You think the same thing about rape. "There is, after all, nothing more natural than rape. But no one would argue that rape is good, or compatible with a civil society, because it may have had evolutionary advantages for our ancestors" (91). As with rape, so with religion. May have been useful once, but not anymore.

You lament "the failure of our schools to announce the death of God in a way that each generation can understand" (91). That failure is a necessary one. Mankind was created by God, and despite man's sin, we cannot shake the reality of that createdness from ourselves. Public schools certainly can't do it. Nothing can alter the fundamental way in which God has configured the world. Arguments with gravity are difficult to maintain.

And this leads to the second part of this last installment. Bits and pieces of what I am about to say have been sprinkled throughout this short book, but I wanted to make sure that at some point I stated the whole thing together in some sort of coherent fashion. I said earlier that mankind is all screwed up. But this is not because we crawled out of the primordial ooze, not yet arriving at our evolutionary destination. In the gospel, the Christian Church declares that man has fallen from his first estate. In other words, we believe in *devolution*, not evolution.

God created us upright, to have fellowship with Him, and we rejected this—rebelling for the sake of autonomy. A desire to maintain that same autonomy is manifest throughout your book. You want to think the way you want to think. When Adam and Eve were being tempted in the Garden, they saw that the fruit was good for food, pleasant to the eyes, and suitable to make them wise. This threefold temptation corresponded to something the apostle John wrote many centuries later—Christians are charged to avoid worldliness, and this means avoiding the lust of the flesh, the lust of the eyes, and the pride of life (1 John 2:16). The lust of the flesh corresponds to the fruit as food, the lust of the eyes corresponds to its pleasing appearance, and the pride of life (the real center of all the mischief) corresponds to the autonomous desire to be like God.

When Adam rebelled against God, the entire human race was plunged into sin. We were not only hurled headlong into a great ocean of sins and sinning, but into the very condition of sin itself. Every aspect of our being was polluted in this fall. We do not just *do* bad things; we do them because we *are* bad people. Much of your book pointed out many of the bad things we do. You attributed this to "religion," but it would be much closer to the mark to attribute it to "people." You are quite right about one thing though. Religion doesn't fix the problem, and in many cases, it just compounds the problem. Two inches of snow on a dung heap can look pretty nice, but it doesn't address the deeper problem. So if we sinful men go left, we sin on the left. If we go right, we sin on the right. If we become atheists, we sin there. If we become Jehovah's Witnesses, we sin there. *Wherever we go, there we are.* The generic category of "religion" cannot help us in this anymore than the abstract concept of "medicine" can help us when we are sick. We need *actual* medicine, not the *idea* of medicine. And this is why we need Christ, not religion.

And so, according to the gospel, the entire human race was captured in this state of death. We live out our pathetic lives in this death. But just as the head of our race, Adam, got us into this slavery of sin, so God resolved to provide salvation by the same means. An Adam got us into this, and an Adam was God's choice to get us out. This is why Jesus Christ was born into our race—so He could become the last Adam and the founder of a new humanity. This is what the Christian Church actually *is*—humanity reconstituted in Christ. This may seem to you to be nothing more than an arrogant hyper-sectarianism, but it really is not. This is because the prophets proclaimed that in Christ the entire world would be efficaciously forgiven, delivered, and restored in their humanity. This is not a message for a mystery cult tucked away in a corner somewhere; it is good news for the entire world.

Because of our sinfulness and sins, we all deserved the sentence of death and hell forever. But instead of this, Christ came to offer a glorious exchange. All our sins would be placed on Him, and all His righteousness would be placed on us (2 Cor. 5:21). In its culmination, this transaction occurred at the cross. Jesus died and in that death He embraced the pollutions of a very polluted world. He took onto Himself the wrath and anger of God, and He did this so that in Him we might become the righteousness of God. He gathered up a world full of hatred, adultery, treachery, rape, murder, envy, genocide, religious hypocrisy, atheism, theft, lying, and all forms of arrogant haughtiness, gathered it all to His chest, and disappearing, sank into death.

But what looked like death and sin overwhelming the Messiah was actually the Messiah overwhelming death and sin. That uncanny, numinous moment was actually the death of death in the death of Christ. God determined that our Lord's wonderful sacrifice would be the hinge upon which the new world would turn. Because Jesus rose from the dead, leaving the sin behind Him in the grave, we who have been joined with Him in that death are also joined with Him in His resurrection. And this is what we mean when we refer to what it means to be born again; we are regenerated in order that we

might walk with Him in newness of life. All
the blessings that God is willing to give to
humanity are right *there*, in the death, burial
and resurrection of Jesus Christ. This is the
gospel.

The apostle Paul teaches us in the first
chapter of Romans (1:21) that there are two
particular aspects of the creature's relationship
to God that sinful men want to suppress or
deny. The first is the sovereignty of God,
or, if you like, the *Godness* of God. We have
already covered this earlier in our discussion
of the Asian tsunami and Hurricane Katrina.
God disposes of His creation as He pleases.
But even when it comes to expressions of
God's severity, the apostle talks about it in
a context that sees rebellious men coming
back to Him in repentance (Rom. 11:22–23).
The fundamental orientation of God to our
sinful world is one of redemptive love, not
annihilating wrath (John 3:17). The wrath is
a reality, but the basic expression of it is seen
in the cross, where Jesus suffered the wrath
of God for the sins of His people. Wrath and
love met in the cross, and this is why we as
sinners can be saved. Because of the death of

Jesus, the world is *delivered* from the wrath of God (1 John 2:1–2).

And this leads to the second thing that sinful men want to get away from, which is the obligation to be thankful (Rom. 1:21). One of the principle failings in atheism is that it leaves us with no one to thank for the countless blessings we encounter daily. This extends from trivial things, like the pleasure we get from pulling our socks up, to more amazing gifts, like food, and music, and marriage. And of course, the capstone of all our gratitude is thanksgiving for what the New Testament describes as the "indescribable gift" (2 Cor. 9:15)—the gospel of our Lord Jesus. Jesus died and rose to straighten it all out, and that is what He is doing.

Now I know that if you have read this far, it is probably because you are just "indulging the preacher." But I do want you to know that *I* know that this sounds like gibberish to you. As an argument, I know that it seems beyond strange. "A Jewish carpenter was executed by the authorities of Jerusalem two thousand years ago, and this happened so that our sins could be forgiven?" So why do I repeat it then, *knowing* how strange it sounds to you? Well, the answer is that God has promised to transform the entire world—a multitude beyond all counting was promised to Abraham—as people listen to this particular story being told. And for two thousand years He has been doing exactly that. And so Christians will continue to tell it until He stops fulfilling His word, which means that this is *the* story that will be told to the end of the world.

May the Lord call you to Himself, on the basis of this kind gospel. But whether He does this or not, if we ever meet, I would love to buy you a beer.

TEN BOOKS I RECOMMEND

1. *Orthodoxy* by G.K. Chesteron

2. *Mere Christianity* by C.S. Lewis

3. *Always Ready* by Greg L. Bahnsen

4. *Pushing the Antithesis* edited by Gary DeMar

5. *Clean Water, Red Wine, Broken Bread* by Douglas Wilson

6. *Apologetics to the Glory of God* by John Frame

7. *Knowing God* by J. I. Packer.

8. *The New Atheism and the Erosion of Freedom* by Robert A. Morey

9. *Does God Believe in Atheists?* by John Blanchard

10. *The Real Face of Atheism* by Ravi Zacharias

Douglas Wilson

NOTES

[1]*Books and Culture*, 11:2 (March/April 2005), 22–29.

[2]A careful reading of Mark 7:10 shows that the law is not applied to infants or toddlers. Jesus is addressing adult children.

[3]N.T. Wright, *Colossians and Philemon* (Grand Rapids, MI: Eerdmans, 1986), 164–192.

[4]Peter Leithart, *Deep Comedy* (Moscow, ID: Canon Press, 2006).

[5]Douglas Wilson, *Her Hand in Marriage* (Moscow, ID: Canon Press, 1997), 24ff, 31.

[6]Albert Alschuler, *Law Without Values* (Chicago, IL: University of Chicago Press, 2000), 1.

[7]Alschuler, *Law Without Values*, 1.

[8]Alschuler, *Law Without Values*, 11.

[9]Alschuler, *Law Without Values*, 6.

[10]Alschuler, *Law Without Values*, 23.

[11]Alschuler, *Law Without Values*, 23.

[12]Thomas Kuhn, *The Structure of Scientific Revolutions* (Chicago, IL: University of Chicago Press, 1962).

[13]Richard Weikart, *From Darwin to Hitler* (New York: Palgrave Macmillan, 2004).

Discover more about

AMERICAN VISION

WWW.AMERICANVISION.ORG
1-800-628-9460
3150-A Florence Road
Powder Springs, GA 30127